Forgiveness

THE ART OF LIVING SERIES

Series Editor: Mark Vernon

From Plato to Bertrand Russell philosophers have engaged wide audiences on matters of life and death. *The Art of Living* series aims to open up philosophy's riches to a wider public once again. Taking its lead from the concerns of the ancient Greek philosophers, the series asks the question "How should we live?". Authors draw on their own personal reflections to write philosophy that seeks to enrich, stimulate and challenge the reader's thoughts about their own life.

Clothes *John Harvey*
Commitment *Piers Benn*
Death *Todd May*
Deception *Ziyad Marar*
Distraction *Damon Young*
Faith *Theo Hobson*
Fame *Mark Rowlands*
Forgiveness *Eve Garrard and David McNaughton*
Hunger *Raymond Tallis*
Illness *Havi Carel*
Me *Mel Thompson*
Middle Age *Christopher Hamilton*
Money *Eric Lonergan*
Pets *Erica Fudge*
Science *Steve Fuller*
Sport *Colin McGinn*
Wellbeing *Mark Vernon*
Work *Lars Svendsen*

Forgiveness

Eve Garrard and David McNaughton

ACUMEN

© Eve Garrard & David McNaughton, 2010

Acumen Publishing Limited
4 Saddler Street
Durham
DH1 3NP
www.acumenpublishing.co.uk

ISBN: 978-1-84465-226-6

British Library Cataloguing-in-Publication Data
A catalogue record for this book is available from the British Library.

Typeset in Warnock Pro.
Printed by Ashford Colour Press Ltd, UK.

Contents

Preface

What can you expect to find in this book, and – perhaps just as importantly – what can you *not* expect to find? In these pages, we try to answer two central questions about forgiveness: first, what exactly are we doing when we forgive someone who has wronged us or behaved badly towards us? And second, what reasons are there to forgive, and what reasons are there to withhold forgiveness? Addressing these two questions is the central aim of this book.

People use the term "forgiveness" to cover a number of things. Thus we can talk not only about forgiving wrongdoers, but also about forgiving debts. In this book we are interested only in the first kind of forgiveness, not in the second. This is because to forgive a debt is simply to let the borrower off having to repay the money, with no implication that the borrower has done anything wrong. There are important and interesting questions about whether, for example, advanced industrial nations should forgive the debts owed to them by developing nations, but they won't concern us here, because what we're interested in is the fact that when we forgive a *person*, it must be because we think that they have done something *wrong*, something for which they need forgiveness. It's this forgiving attitude towards wrongdoing that we want to focus on, in order to see more clearly what it involves, and to find out what reasons (if any) there are for adopting it.

Forgiveness is an important theme in many religious traditions, and in the case of Christianity it's absolutely central, it's the focal point. However, we won't specifically discuss religious conceptions of forgiveness in this book. Why not? Well, first, we aren't experts in the various religious traditions, and so we can't really do justice to their doctrines. Second, for many major religious traditions, a central issue is God's forgiveness of our sins. But there are good reasons for thinking that God's forgiveness isn't just like human forgiveness, and that the reasons God might have to forgive sinners aren't the same as the reasons we humans might have to forgive wrongdoers. Pursuing all this would take us too far afield from our central concerns. Finally, and most importantly, we want to see, independently of any particular religious tradition, whether there are good reasons to forgive those who have wronged us. If there are such reasons then all of us, whatever our religious beliefs, have reason to forgive one another. If this is true, it's certainly worth finding out about.

While there is very little about theology in this book, there is a whole chapter on psychological studies of forgiveness. The reason for this is that in recent years many people have made strong and sometimes startling claims about the healing power of forgiveness. Therapists, gurus, television pundits and, of course, the authors of innumerable self-help books have trumpeted the benefits of forgiveness to the forgiver. Forgive, and the burden of rancour and hatred will be lifted from your shoulders; fail to forgive, and you will be trapped in a cycle of resentment, unable to move on and get on with your life. In failing to forgive, it's often claimed, you'll be allowing the perpetrator of the wrong to continue to control your life. Forgive, and you'll free yourself from the role of victim in which the wrongdoer has cast you. No doubt there is some truth in all this, but we should maintain considerable scepticism towards such sweeping and extravagant claims. However, whether or not people's lives do go better if they forgive isn't something that can be settled by thinking about it in an armchair. We need studies to test these claims. As it happens, psychologists have, in recent years, become very interested in just this topic, so we spend some time looking at their studies and experiments to see how well supported those claims are.

With the exception of that one chapter, the rest of the book is pure philosophy. The word "philosophy" conjures up very different pictures in different people. And many suppose that philosophy must, by its very nature, be abstruse, difficult, and even technical. Sometimes philosophy is indeed like that, but it needn't always be. Philosophers are looking for two things that any reflective person seeks: understanding and justification. In this case, we want first to understand clearly what forgiveness is and so, of course, also what it is not. Once we're clear what forgiveness is, we want to consider when we are justified in withholding forgiveness and when we may, and perhaps should, grant it. That is, we try to be as clear as we can both about the case for forgiveness and about the case against it. In doing this, philosophers are not engaging in some special activity – an eccentric hobby – that only they are interested in. Rather, they are asking questions that have been asked by anyone who has ever been wronged and has thought about how she should respond. These questions are also often asked, in pain and regret, by those who have wronged others and now feel remorse about what they have done. One way or another that surely includes all of us. Philosophy is simply the activity of thinking through these questions clearly and carefully, in order to test the various answers that have been given and to see which ones stand up to scrutiny. And that is what we try to do here.

Acknowledgements

We have benefited from discussions with many people over the years, including Anthony Bash, Thomas Brudholm, David Copp, Frank Fincham, David Garrard, Norman Geras, Charles Griswold, Kirk Ludwig, Cynthia Macdonald, Graham Macdonald, Michael McKenna, James McNulty, Jeffrie Murphy, Piers Rawling, David Speller, Eleonore Stump and Brandon Warmke. We have also received helpful comments from audiences at the universities of Florida State, Reading and Virginia, and at various conferences, including the Florida Philosophical Association and a conference on forgiveness at the University of Oslo.

1. The debate about forgiveness

A man lies in the rubble of a building that has been blown apart by a bomb. He will survive, but his daughter crushed there beside him will not. He holds her hand as she lies dying. Later, when he has been rescued, he says that he forgives the terrorists who have killed his daughter; he wishes them no ill.

Many people would regard the unconditional forgiveness that is offered in this case as absolutely admirable, even saintly, in its ability to rise above the hatred and enmity that would be a natural response to so terrible an event. (In fact, many people did so regard it, since this is the case of Gordon Wilson, who lost his daughter in the Enniskillen bombing in Northern Ireland). But some would not and did not find it admirable, thinking that forgiveness isn't the right response, the *appropriate* response, to those who deliberately choose to murder innocent and helpless victims. Whether forgiveness is always appropriate and admirable is something that people disagree about, sometimes quite strongly, and often they find it hard to understand the position of those who don't share their views on this troubling topic. On the one hand, some say, how can we fail to admire a person who rises above rancour and hatred and vengefulness, and offers goodwill to those who have injured him so badly? On the other hand, comes the rejoinder, how can we fail to be angry and outraged at the offender's terrible crimes, and why should we pretend that they don't matter and that a just punishment for them isn't important?

This is an issue that matters in everybody's life. Its importance ranges from the details of an individual's life to geopolitical forces that impinge on whole nations and may make the difference between war and peace. We all have occasion to consider forgiving others, or to hope to be forgiven by them: certainly in our private affairs, often at the public level too. The debate about forgiveness touches on large questions about how we should stand towards all our fellow humans, and the view we take of it can colour our whole lives, for good or ill. People feel strongly about it, and rightly so; it does, after all, raise the question of how we should respond to human wrongdoing, which itself ranges from minor unkindness to horrific and sickening atrocities committed against thousands or even millions of human beings. But our strong feelings, although entirely appropriate, aren't enough to settle the question about whether or when we should forgive wrongdoers. They aren't enough to guide us on this issue, partly because they don't speak with a single voice. People's feelings about forgiveness differ from one culture to another; even within a single culture they differ from one individual to another; and sometimes even within the one individual feelings about forgiveness may fluctuate wildly from one occasion to another. Strength of feeling won't settle the question of whether we should forgive wrongdoers and, if so, in what circumstances. Only a consideration of the arguments, both for and against forgiveness, will help us come to some more stable and well-supported position on this matter.

This book aims to provide those arguments, and to examine their strengths and weaknesses. In this chapter we're going to give a broad outline of the nature of the debate about forgiveness, and indicate some of the main areas where people disagree. In Chapter 2 we'll focus on the case against forgiveness: on arguments that claim forgiveness is not always desirable, and indeed is sometimes morally wrong. Chapter 3 will examine a third possibility, neither hatred nor forgiveness, and consider whether this provides a satisfactory response to human wrongdoing. In Chapter 4, we'll look at some of the empirical research done by psychologists working in this area, and consider what we can learn from them. In Chapter 5, we'll examine in some detail the nature of forgiveness, and see whether this more complex understanding can help to meet the criticisms that have been levelled at it. And finally, in Chapter 6 we'll look at the positive arguments in favour of forgiveness, and try to assess their strength and persuasiveness.

Forgiveness and therapy

Forgiveness – the giving and withholding of it – is something we're all involved in, one way or another. All of us have had the experience of being wronged by others, an experience that very naturally produces resentment and ill will towards the offender. And sooner or later we have to decide whether to maintain that resentment and ill will, or whether to abandon it and replace it with something different: perhaps indifference and forgetting, or perhaps something closer to goodwill and reconciliation – closer, in fact, to forgiveness. It's also true that all of us have had the experience of wronging others (at least, if there is anyone who hasn't had that experience, they don't need to be reading this book, and can close it at once). A very normal feature of knowing that you've done something really wrong is wishing that you could go back and change things, and failing that (since changing the past is impossible) wishing that you could somehow change the meaning of your action, alter the significance of what you've done. Being forgiven by the person whom you've wronged does somehow or other seem to achieve that, at least to some extent, so it's not surprising that people who acknowledge that they really have done serious wrong very often seek forgiveness from their victims.

That is what happened to Eric Lomax: he was a prisoner of the Japanese during the Second World War, working on the infamous Burma railway; and during his imprisonment he, along with many

3

others, was hideously and disgustingly and mercilessly tortured. After the war was over, he experienced the terrible psychological disturbances common among those who have been tortured. (As Jean Améry, a survivor of Auschwitz, said, a person who has been tortured remains tortured forever.) For decades afterwards, Lomax continued to suffer and to hate those who had deliberately and ingeniously inflicted so much pain on him and his comrades. He sought out no further contact with them, but was glad to learn that two had been executed as war criminals, and that his own testimony had contributed to their fate. However, after many years he heard news of one of his erstwhile tormentors who had survived the war, and who had spent the years thereafter in attempting to atone for his horrific activities. Now that he could identify this man, Lomax at first hoped to harm him, perhaps to kill him, to avenge some small part of the nightmare into which he had been plunged. But after contact was established, he found that in the light of his torturer's remorse, "anger drained away; in its place came a welling of compassion for both Nagase and me, coupled with a deep sense of sadness and regret. ... Forgiveness became more than an abstract idea: it was now a real possibility."

Eric Lomax had every reason to hate and despise his terrible tormentor; in the end, however, he found forgiveness not only possible but actually welcome. But even in the light of that story of redemptive forgiveness, we might well wonder what exactly is so good about forgiving a fanatical torturer. Why *should* we forgive people who have done terrible things? Isn't it preferable to hold on to our sense of how wrong they were, and continue to hate them for their evil acts, instead of pretending that somehow they didn't happen or don't really matter? When someone has enacted nightmarish atrocities, should their later apologies somehow wipe out the horror of what they did? Why should we think that it is in the end preferable, as Lomax found, to relinquish our hatred and vengefulness and turn towards reconciliation?

Therapeutic

Those who favour forgiveness often claim that its value resides in the way in which it frees and strengthens both the forgiver and the forgiven one: it allows us to escape the shackles of the wrongful past and to move on to a future that isn't dominated by bitterness and resentment. Forgiveness, they think, is a light shining in a dark world: it's a gesture not only of kindness but also of generosity, and the free gift that it offers somehow benefits the forgiver as well as the wrongdoer – here, if anywhere, it is at least as good to give as to receive.

In support of this view, popular culture in the West has for quite some time been saturated with self-help books and television shows about forgiveness and reconciliation. And nearly all of them convey the same message: forgiveness is good for everyone. It's good for you and it's good for others; you need to let go of the anger and move on. A cursory glance at Google will bring up thousands of links to websites offering us various approaches to forgiveness: "Forgive and Forget With Our Make Your Peace Toolkit"; "Self-Help Techniques (For I Give)"; "Forgiveness – Free Self-Help Software for Inner Peace"; "Self Help Portal 4 U: Forgiveness and Empowerment"; and (a special favourite) "Institute for Radical Forgiveness Slashes Prices – Affordable Self-Help During Difficult Times".

Possible to do this without forgiving?

The desire to make a buck out of commending forgiveness to others may not be very admirable, but the prevalence of these offers suggests that there's a ready market for them, that a great many people do think that there's something very desirable about forgiveness. The central idea here seems to be that forgiveness is *therapeutic*, that people who have been wronged will feel better about themselves and about their lives if they forgive those who have wronged them, that the act of forgiveness will make them feel, and be, more powerful. There is certainly something to be said for this therapeutic view of forgiveness: the experience of forgiving a long-hated enemy can be absolutely cathartic, and when the burden of resentment slips off your shoulders it can feel thoroughly liberating.

but is this forgiveness really?

5

But in truth much of this self-help advocacy is very shallow: it fails to address the realities of terrible wrongdoing and what it does, and means, to its victims. Think of a woman, a mother of young children, whose husband has an affair with her best friend. Her overwhelming sense of betrayal by the two people whom she had most reason to trust may be focused not exclusively on herself at all, but also and perhaps primarily on her children, and how they have been betrayed and damaged by those who should have cared for and protected them. To forgive her husband and her friend may seem like a further betrayal of those children, a further neglect and diminishing and glossing over of the harm done to them.

On a larger scale, consider the experience of the victims of the European wars in the middle of the twentieth century, and of too many elsewhere in the world today: attacked, tortured, their children raped and murdered, their whole way of life irrevocably destroyed. To tell them to forgive and to achieve closure is not just to tell them to adopt an attitude of goodwill towards those very murderers and torturers; it seems to amount to telling them to move on from the ruined and lost lives of their children, and to leave such things behind them. It's not surprising that many such victims feel that forgiveness is not only emotionally beyond them, but would also amount to a failure to take their losses and, even more importantly, those who were lost with sufficient seriousness. Forgiveness in these circumstances can come to seem a way of dismissing the suffering of the victims, of failing to keep faith with them, especially with those who are dead and can no longer raise their voices against their tormentors.

So we need to see if there are other reasons for forgiving wrong-doers, apart from the therapeutic effects that are so often touted in its favour. And a good way to start the search for these reasons is to look at the broad historical context in which our ideas of forgiveness have developed.

6

The historical context

It's not really surprising that forgiveness gets such a good press, at least in Western culture, shaped as it has been by the tremendous influence of Christianity and its focus upon wrongdoers and their need for forgiveness. In Christianity the sinner is a central figure, and his need for redemption from his sins is what drives the great core narrative of the incarnation of Christ and his sacrifice on the cross. The central texts of Christianity, the Gospels, are the bringing of good news to humanity, and the good news is that through Christ's actions our sins are forgiven us. This picture of the world and its meaning is one that assumes we all realize how sinful we are, how much we fail to live up to our moral standards, how readily we harm and wrong others, and how much in need of rescue we are from this terrible condition of irremediable wrongdoing. According to Christianity such rescue is possible: forgiveness is the means of redemption from our sins. Since we are all sinners we are all in need of forgiveness; and crucially (according to Christianity) if we hope for forgiveness from God then first we must forgive others who have offended against us.

This picture of the human condition, with the wrongdoer at centre stage and forgiveness as the source of salvation for all of us, has in the past been enormously influential, at least at the level of rhetoric; what people, including Christians, *say* about the universal need for and desirability of forgiveness has often been very different from what they actually *do* about and towards those who they think have wronged them. Christian practice has often failed to live up to this elevated account of how we should treat our fellow sinners. But forgiveness as an ideal has been, and for many people remains, an intensely attractive moral commitment, and it's easy to see why: if we feel ourselves burdened with the guilt of our wrongdoings, then the idea of forgiveness, both human and even more divine, offers relief from that weight of guilt, and perhaps even the possibility of escape from our enduring propensity to harm and wrong others. On this picture, when we forgive our enemies we imitate, insofar as we are able, the goodness and generosity and loving-kindness of God; we reach out beyond our desperately flawed condition to some better way of being.

Appeal to the Christian religious tradition may not, however, cut very much ice with those who are adherents of different religions, and may seem totally irrelevant to people who have no religious commitments at all. Nonetheless many people, of all religions and none, agree that human beings are morally imperfect in some very important ways. This agreement isn't really surprising: the most cursory glance at human history, religious and irreligious alike, is enough to reveal the depths of moral degradation that human beings have been ready to plumb again and again throughout the centuries. The bloody and murderous record of the twentieth century alone is enough to show the persistent streak of evil running through human history. The mass murders, tortures and genocides of that terrible century (not to mention those already being clocked up in its successor), and the extent to which ordinary people were and are drawn into these pitiless activities, leaves it almost impossible for us to think of human nature as essentially innocent and good. Although there are, of course, many aspects of human nature and history that are benign and indeed admirable, it's no longer plausible (if it ever was) to suppose that we are at heart entirely benevolent and sociable creatures; there's a dark surd deep in our psychology that repeatedly leads almost all of us to do things that we know are wrong, and which in some cases amount to hideous atrocities.

In this view of human nature there's the material for a secular analogue of the religious doctrine of original sin. We don't have to believe in some primal act of disobedience in the Garden of Eden, tainting all future generations, in order to think that the human condition is one in which very few of us go through life without doing wrong, without sometimes harming others in ways that simply can't be justified. The reasons for this may be buried deep in our evolutionary past, or alternatively they may be an inevitable outcome of our distinctively human ability to choose for ourselves between good and evil. But whatever explanation we want to give of human wrongdoing, its persistence means that forgiveness is going to be a significant issue for a secular outlook on the world, just as it is for a religious outlook. And anyone who has felt the weight of guilt, who has taken her own wrongdoing seriously and has accepted her own responsibility for it, will already know that the possibility of forgiveness, of making a new start, isn't something to be lightly dismissed.

Before we go any further, there's one view that we need to deal with, since if it's correct, it may seem to make forgiveness unnecessary. This is the view that guilt is a bad thing, that it's all just wasted energy, that it's a pathological hangover from a puritanical past and that we'd all be much better off without it. And if guilt is unnecessary and undesirable, then it might be thought that forgiveness is likewise redundant.

Right enough, some guilt is pathological: some people are consumed with guilt for offences that are far too minor (if indeed they exist at all) to warrant such misery and angst. People would certainly be much better off without that kind of misplaced guilt. But the fact that guilt is *sometimes* misplaced doesn't show that it's *always* misplaced. The man who sexually abuses a child in his care, and thereby makes a horror of her childhood and perhaps damages all her future chances of happiness, may eventually come to see the nature of the wrong he has done to her. Are his feelings of guilt then misplaced? Would it be better if he regarded his behaviour as just part of the rich tapestry of human experience, and felt no regret or remorse about his actions? Would it be better if the woman who was a concentration camp guard, and who was instrumental in the torture and murder of other innocent women, looked on her past actions with an equable eye as being all right at the time? People who are serious about morality – that is, about the needs and rights of others – will inevitably and correctly feel guilty if they violate those rights and needs. It's true that there are plenty of people, particularly in adolescence, who will *say* that they don't care about morality, but they usually turn out to have remarkably definite views about oppression or injustice (which are essentially moral categories), especially when it's committed against them or against groups about whom they feel strongly. People who really don't take any aspect of morality seriously, who genuinely don't care how much they hurt or exploit others, aren't so much free spirits as psychopaths who are cut off from most of the relationships that illuminate and make valuable a human life, and in fact there are remarkably few such people.

So if we take morality seriously, as we should, then guilt is going to be part of the package deal, as is moral praise and admiration; if we want the latter, then we have to have the former too. And with guilt comes the possibility of, and the need for, forgiveness. But is it always right to forgive wrongdoers? Is forgiveness as good as it's cracked up to be?

Current advocacy of forgiveness

As we have seen, the current answer to that question is very often an unqualified and uncritical yes. Victims of the most terrible crimes who forgive their perpetrators are greatly praised by the media and by cultural and religious commentators, whereas those victims who publicly refuse to forgive their tormentors are often the objects of a very ambiguous response: we feel at once sympathetic to them for their bitterness about the mistreatment (or worse) that they underwent at the hands of the offenders, and also, perhaps rather covertly, critical of their failure to rise above their grievances (this very revealing locution shows how much we think of forgiveness as being higher and better than alternative responses to wrongdoing). We tell these unforgiving victims that they need to let go of the bitterness, to move on from their absorption in the events in which they were victimized, to act generously and put the past behind them so that there may be reconciliation and peace. Forgiveness is thought to be admirable, even beautiful; and the alternative of resentment and desire for retribution is often seen as being crude and primitive and morally regressive. Indeed the desire for retributive justice is often regarded as indistinguishable from a desire for revenge, and revenge is generally thought to be morally deplorable, a hangover from a more primitive and ferocious, perhaps even premoral, response to wrongdoing.

A central feature of contemporary boosterism about forgiveness is that it focuses on the benefits it will bring to the forgiver, rather than to the person forgiven. On this picture of forgiveness, if the victim of wrongdoing fails to forgive this will lead to her being trapped in the past, her life still dominated by the offence and the offender. The woman who is still, perhaps years after the event, filled with resentment and hatred for the husband and friend who have betrayed her isn't yet free from what happened. Her continuing anger (it is thought) leaves her still in the power of the wrongdoer; he continues to hurt her through her own lingering emotions of resentment and hostility, which bind her to the past with all its burden of victimization. Forgiveness, on the other hand (so it is said), will liberate the victim from both the wrongdoer and the wrong itself: she will be able to rise above her victimhood and move on. On this therapeutic view, victims need, for their own good, to get over the wrongs that have been inflicted on them; and forgiveness is what enables them to do this.

Now there certainly is some truth in this. Some people who have been wronged continue to brood over their injuries to their own detriment, so that their sense of grievance swallows up their lives, and the consequent bitterness taints all their other experiences. In

11

some cases it's hard to see how the victims could avoid this; the mother of a child who has been abused and murdered may find all of the rest of her life subsumed under her pursuit of retribution for the murder of her child, and indeed the devastation of her life is another charge to be laid at the door of the murderer. One tragic example of this was Ann West, whose daughter was tortured and killed by the Moors murderers Myra Hindley and Ian Brady.

> Ann West's daughter Lesley Ann Downey was killed by Myra Hindley and Ian Brady, after [they abducted] ... her on Boxing Day 1964. ...
>
> Lesley Ann Downey was 10 years old when she was kidnapped by Hindley and Brady from a fairground in Manchester. She was stripped, gagged, sexually assaulted and strangled before being buried in a shallow grave on Lancashire's bleak Saddleworth Moor. Mrs West saw photographs taken by her daughter's killers showing Lesley Ann tied up and helpless in the hours leading up to her death. She also had to listen to Brady and Hindley's tape recording of her daughter's cries for mercy. Mrs West was adamant that it was Hindley's hands which squeezed out her daughter's final breath and had threatened to kill her on many occasions. ...
>
> She also vowed to haunt Hindley from beyond the grave, saying: "I will still be a thorn in her side after I pass on, I will haunt that woman for the rest of her life." ...
>
> Her doctors said that the years of stress had contributed to the cancer which affected her ovaries, breast, bowel and liver. ...
>
> But the illness did not stop her campaigning and in 1997 she visited a High Court hearing on Hindley's future in a wheelchair. At the time she told BBC News she was determined that Hindley should end her life behind bars.
>
> (http://news.bbc.co.uk/1/hi/uk/276809.stm
> [accessed July 2010])

Who among us would have the courage, or the gall, to tell such a mother that she must forgive her child's destroyer, that she must move on beyond the past and its traumas, even if we can see that her life might go better if she did manage to forgive? There are some situations in which making one's own life go better doesn't seem to be the most important thing, a point to which we'll return later in the book.

There's also a further and different problem with the therapeutic conception of forgiveness: it seems to miss out an essential aspect of forgiveness, namely, that it's something that the forgiver, the victim, *gives*, and she gives it *to the wrongdoer*. On the therapeutic picture, forgiveness is all about the *victim*, while the victim's relation to the wrongdoer drops out as virtually irrelevant. In so far as benefits to anyone else are mentioned they are usually benefits to people other than the wrongdoer; so, for example, forgiveness is sometimes recommended because it will make the victim an easier person to live with for her friends and relatives, or because it will end the cycle of violence and hence prevent the creation of yet more victims.

All of these may be desirable consequences of forgiveness, but they don't really go to the heart of what's going on here. The wrongdoer seems to have virtually disappeared from the story. But we characteristically think of forgiveness, and forgivers, as being *generous*, and that's hard to understand if we think of forgiveness as primarily benefiting the forgiver, the person who was the victim of the original wrongdoing.

In one of the earliest examples of unconditional forgiveness available to us, the biblical story of the prodigal son, we can see an understanding of forgiveness that owes nothing to the therapeutic conception. In fact, this early parable reveals a great deal both about the nature of forgiveness and about why it's morally problematic, why some people regard it as morally wrong to forgive in certain circumstances.

13

Once a man had two sons. The younger son said to his father, "Give me my share of the property". So the father divided his property between his two sons. Not long after that, the younger son packed up everything he owned and left for a foreign country, where he wasted all his money in wild living. He had spent everything, when a bad famine spread through that whole land. Soon he had nothing to eat.

He went to work for a man in that country, and the man sent him out to take care of his pigs. He would have been glad to eat what the pigs were eating, but no one gave him a thing. Finally, he came to his senses and said, "My father's workers have plenty to eat, and here I am, starving to death! I will go to my father and say to him, 'Father, I have sinned against God in heaven and against you. I am no longer good enough to be called your son. Treat me like one of your workers'."

The younger son got up and started back to his father. But when he was still a long way off, his father saw him and felt sorry for him. He ran to his son and hugged and kissed him. The son said, "Father, I have sinned against God in heaven and against you. I am no longer good enough to be called your son". But his father said to the servants, "Hurry and bring the best clothes and put them on him. Give him a ring for his finger and sandals for his feet. Get the best calf and prepare it, so we can eat and celebrate. This son of mine was dead, but has now come back to life. He was lost and has now been found". And they began to celebrate.

(Luke 15:11–24)

The father who forgives his spendthrift layabout of a son isn't thinking of himself, or his grievances, or his own psychological condition at all; all his attention is focused on the needs of his son, and the recovery of his relationship with him. It's worth noting that in this story the generosity that is so notable a feature of forgiveness is well to the fore in the father, but not in the brother, whose main focus is on issues of justice and fair treatment. In the response of the careful brother we find some of the main objections to forgiveness being clearly articulated:

> The older son had been out in the field. But when he came near the house, he heard the music and dancing. So he called one of the servants over and asked, "What's going on here?" The servant answered, "Your brother has come home safe and sound, and your father ordered us to kill the best calf". The older brother got so angry that he would not even go into the house. His father came out and begged him to go in. But he said to his father, "For years I have worked for you like a slave and have always obeyed you. But you have never even given me a little goat, so that I could give a dinner for my friends. This other son of yours wasted your money on prostitutes. And now that he has come home, you ordered the best calf to be killed for a feast". His father replied, "My son, you are always with me, and everything I have is yours. But we should be glad and celebrate! Your brother was dead, but he is now alive. He was lost and has now been found".   (Luke 15:25–32)

It's hard not to feel sympathy for the careful brother, who is angered at the sheer unfairness of his treatment compared to that of the wayward and prodigal son. It *is* unfair and inequitable: the brother stays home and does all the work, and the wayward son is forgiven for his idleness and selfishness, and gets what he certainly doesn't deserve. By comparison, the careful brother does badly, and this is unjust, since he did nothing to deserve disadvantageous treatment from his father. However, the brother's demand for equity throws into very stark relief the unforced generosity of the father's joyful forgiveness, and we can see that in such cases we're faced with a contrast between equity and justice on the one

15

hand, and generosity and love on the other. Both these concerns make powerful claims on our moral attention, but the significant thing here is that the biblical story does not recommend or display forgiveness as being of primarily therapeutic value for the victim who forgives, but rather as being the generous and loving response to the recovery of a person and a relationship that had been thought to be dead. The value that the father places on his wayward son is unaffected by his misdeeds, and forgiveness is presented as the appropriate response to a person who, although a wrongdoer, nonetheless remains valuable and valued.

If we're to understand forgiveness properly we'll need an account of the reasons for forgiveness that will show us why we think of it as a kind of generosity, and the therapeutic account doesn't seem to do that: it's too focused on how forgiveness does the forgiver good. But when people act so as to benefit themselves, we don't normally think that counts as being generous, even if their actions do benefit others as well. Think of the football star who earns hundreds of thousands of pounds exercising his skills, and in doing so benefits others by bringing enormous interest and enjoyment to many thousands of spectators. We may be pleased about this, but we don't normally think of the footballer as *generous* in displaying his skill on the pitch (and earning mega-bucks each time he plays). Thinking of forgiveness as primarily good for the forgiver and those close to her doesn't help us to see why it's a generous thing to do – but generosity is a central part of our idea of forgiveness. We need a better account of what exactly it is we're doing when we forgive, and why that's a good thing in itself.

Forgiveness as a virtue

"Boosterists" about forgiveness advocate it in ways that can be both superficial and distorting. For them, learning to forgive is a goal of self-development, like overcoming shyness, dealing with loss, or getting over rejection. It helps you do better in life, and be more successful at whatever it is you want to do. There's nothing wrong with that, of course, but there's nothing especially moral about it either. This picture of forgiveness fails to show why it's morally admirable, why we think of it as a virtue, why it involves a generosity of spirit that's quite unlike our concerns to become more successful in reaching our goals in life.

Putting forgiveness in such company sells it short. Proper forgiveness is far more than merely a psychological exercise to make the victim feel better. We see this when we consider the striking and moving examples of forgiveness already mentioned, such as Gordon Wilson forgiving the Enniskillen bombers or Eric Lomax forgiving his Japanese torturer. These are cases that allow us to see forgiveness as a moral achievement, an expression of a difficult but admirable attitude to wrongdoing, in which we respond to disrespect or even hate with goodwill or even love. In short, forgivingness can be thought of as a *virtue* – an admirable feature of a person's character; and like the other virtues, it may take much effort both to acquire and to maintain. Where the offence was profound, forgiving may be a heroic or even saintly act, one that goes well beyond what we can normally expect of people. So here we have the second kind of reason in favour of forgiveness: it expresses humanity, forbearance, compassion – that is, it displays an attitude towards the offender that we may feel is what we ought to show towards all members of the human race. This compassion, this goodwill, is in many people's eyes exemplary: it is what we should offer to all our fellow humans, and the ability to show this attitude even to those who have harmed us is especially desirable and creditable.

Humanity and compassion are among the greatest virtues that people can have. How much more terrible our already terrible world would be if such traits were entirely lacking in us. Forgiveness draws on, and displays, just those characteristics that we can see are central to our humanity; our reason to forgive people is the same as our reason to be humane and compassionate, and forgiveness is admirable because it evinces these traits.

It's true that the virtue of being a forgiving person may indeed (like any of the other virtues such as honesty or courage) make your life go better: it may be good for the forgiver as well as for the offender who gets forgiven. But the person who is truly forgiving doesn't have her own good as her goal; she isn't primarily thinking of herself at all at the point of forgiveness: she's focusing on the wrongdoer instead. And this aspect of forgiveness takes us straight to the fact that attractive though it is, there's also a serious problem with forgiveness, so much so that some people quite reasonably doubt whether forgiveness really is a virtue at all. What they doubt is whether it's morally appropriate to focus on the wrongdoer in this way, to give up ill will towards him and adopt instead a generous attitude of benign goodwill. Why is it right to show compassion and goodwill towards a wrongdoer? He doesn't deserve it, and why should we give people something that they really don't deserve, especially since there are lots of innocent people around who would be far more appropriate objects of our generosity and compassion? Surely, we might think, wrongdoers deserve the hostility that we naturally feel towards them; surely as a matter of *fairness* we should reserve our friendship and goodwill for those who have behaved well towards their fellow human beings? (Here we can see the force of the careful brother's views in the story of the prodigal son.)

To sum up, forgiveness is well thought of in our post-Christian culture, and the recommendation commonly given for it is that it's good for the victim to forgive the wrongdoer. But this isn't always true, and in any case the good of the victim isn't always the most important thing in the victim's eyes. Furthermore, this therapeutic conception of forgiveness doesn't help us to understand why it's a virtue, and why it's considered to be generous to forgive an enemy. A very different reason in support of forgiveness is that it involves humanity and compassion towards the wrongdoer. Many people think that this is a model of how we ought to treat all our fellow humans, and it's especially admirable to adopt this attitude towards someone who has treated you badly, and whom you would be justified in hating. Forgiveness is generous in that it's a gift that the victim gives to the undeserving offender, and it's admirable in that it displays the virtues of humanity, compassion and generosity in circumstances in which these virtues may be difficult to practise. But there are problems with this view of forgiveness: it can be seen as erosive of justice, as failing to consider what people deserve, and as unfairly focusing attention and goodwill on the wrongdoers rather than on the far more deserving victims.

Although there's a lot to be said for forgiveness, there's also a lot to be said for the other side. It's easy to develop a rosy and romantic picture of forgiveness in which all conflicts are resolved by universal goodwill, and everyone sits down together in universal harmony and agrees to overlook the past. But the real-life situations in which the issue of forgiveness actually arises aren't much like that idealized picture; instead, they're haunted by the memory of undeserved harms, and sometimes they're populated by entirely unrepentant offenders facing victims who are still suffering the effects of the sometimes hideous wrongs that have been done to them, and who are quite understandably gripped by a fully justified resentment. In these situations forgiveness is something that's intellectually and emotionally *difficult*, and arguments against forgiveness take on considerable intuitive and rational force. We won't be in a position to properly understand what's good about forgiveness unless we take a closer look at the arguments against it. The strength of these arguments is enough to make those who have doubts about forgiveness think that it's a morally inadequate response – perhaps even a morally contemptible response – to the facts of human wrongdoing. This hostile view of forgiveness is what we must now turn to consider.

2. The case against forgiveness

During the Second World War a young Jew, Simon, is struggling to stay alive in a German prison camp in Poland. His family have been murdered by the Nazis, he himself is starving and worked well-nigh to death, and day after day he watches his fellow inmates die. One day he is taken by the camp guards to the bedside of a patient in the local military hospital, a young S.S. officer who has suffered terrible burns in combat. The officer's head is completely bandaged over, but although he can't see, he can still speak and hear. He seems close to death, but is apparently determined to speak to Simon on his own, and dismisses everyone else from the room. The young Nazi then explains to Simon that he has something on his conscience – he was instrumental in the deliberate burning alive of hundreds of Jews, including women and children. He has demanded Simon's presence in order to ask for his forgiveness, precisely because Simon is Jewish. Simon sits in silence as he hears this story, and listens to the death-bed request for forgiveness from a man who has hideously tortured and killed innocents, and has knowingly furthered the Nazi project of genocide. After a time, Simon silently gets up and walks away, back to the guards and the camp (recounted by Simon Wiesenthal in *The Sunflower*, 25–55).

Was Simon's withholding of forgiveness justified in his circumstances? In any circumstances? Are there cases where we can say outright that it's not only permissible to withhold forgiveness, but that we *ought* to withhold it: that forgiveness is actually the wrong thing to do?

In this chapter, we'll take a closer look at the considerations that count against forgiveness, the reasons why people think that sometimes it's wrong to forgive. It's tempting to think that all the *moral* arguments are on the side of forgiveness, and that the refusal to forgive is driven only by the primitive psychological satisfactions of revenge. But this is a hopelessly crude and shallow picture of what can be involved in refusing to forgive. Yes, it's true that in some cases the refusal to forgive results from an overwhelming desire for, and determination to inflict, revenge. But sometimes far more complex, and more morally significant, considerations are in play, and these shouldn't be overlooked.

What is forgiveness?

In order to see the strength of the case against forgiveness, we must first consider just what forgiveness amounts to. What is involved in forgiving an offender? What does it take to have genuinely forgiven someone who has done you wrong?

People sometimes talk about forgiveness as "wiping the slate clean", as removing everything that has been caused by the offence, and returning matters to where they were before it took place. But if this means that when we forgive we must forget the crime, or behave as if it had never happened, or allow it to make no difference to how the offender is to be treated, then there often seems to be something deeply wrong with that. A mother whose child has been murdered can't just forget the crime, nor would it be right for her (or anyone else) to refuse to let the crime make any difference to how the murderer is to be treated; for a start, it might be important to alter the circumstances in which the murderer could come into contact with other children. Nonetheless, although she couldn't and shouldn't wipe the slate clean, it would be possible for such a mother to forgive her child's murderer (although psychologically, of course, it would be desperately difficult for her to do so.)

"Wiping the slate clean" doesn't capture what's at the heart of forgiveness, because forgiveness is possible, and may be desirable, even where wiping the slate clean isn't. We'll get a better understanding of what forgiveness is if we focus instead on what it rules out: that is, on the states of mind that can't coexist with forgiveness, the feelings and attitudes we'll have to abandon if we're to forgive. We all know that forgiveness involves overcoming something in ourselves, some aspect of our natural response to being wronged. So what are the states of mind that wrongdoing is liable to produce in us, and which of them do we have to overcome in order to forgive someone?

Common, and very understandable, reactions by victims towards offenders include anger, resentment, indignation, rancour, contempt, bitterness, malice, and a range of other negative attitudes. Suppose I have a neighbour I've always found it hard to get on with. He keeps complaining about my family's perfectly ordinary behaviour: he objects to the sound of the children laughing and playing in the garden, saying it's intrusively noisy. And he particularly objects to the dog barking, even though she hardly ever does so; she's really a very quiet and inoffensive dog, who only barks with excitement when the children are playing with her. We're all very fond of her; she's a very sweet and unaggressive animal. But one day my neighbour runs over, and kills, my much-loved dog. It's pretty obvious that this was deliberate. Along with my grief for the loved animal, I'll be consumed with anger about the killing: I'll feel indignation – no, *outrage* – at my neighbour's readiness to harm an innocent beast, and at his lack of concern for normal standards of decent behaviour. I'll resent his treating me and my dog as if our interests were utterly unimportant, as if we didn't count for anything at all. My opinion of the neighbour will of course plummet, and I'll be very ready to tell others what a horrible person he is, and hope that they dislike him on account of this. I'll despise his heartless callousness and insensitivity, and I'll be very pleased if he gets his comeuppance, either at my hands or at the hands of anyone else who's prepared to treat him as he deserves. And if something bad happens to him unconnected to his maltreatment of my dog – perhaps some natural disaster or disease – I may well feel pleased, and talk of "poetic justice", and think that he deserves to suffer, given his vile behaviour.

These negative states of mind are a quite typical range of responses to wrongdoing, and many of them (although not all) are incompatible with forgiveness. Wishing harm to someone, relishing the discomfort and pain that he suffers, just can't go along with forgiving him. Broadly speaking, it's those states of mind that involve *ill will* towards the offender that need to be overcome if we're to forgive. But negative states don't all involve ill will: indignation, for example, need not, since there's no contradiction in saying that I still feel indignant when I think about someone's behaviour, but nonetheless I've personally forgiven him, and now wish him well. Resentment, however, and rancour commonly do involve ill will, and malice invariably does. I can't say without self-contradiction that I hope that things go badly for the offender, and I'll really enjoy it if they do, but all the same I've forgiven him. So it looks as if forgiveness is the overcoming of those negative attitudes that involve ill will, most characteristically resentment and similar emotions.

But that's not quite enough to ensure forgiveness: I can overcome ill will towards an offender without going so far as to actually forgive him. Perhaps the reason I fail to feel any ill will towards an offender is because I've become completely indifferent to him: I no longer care about him or his wrongdoing; I've lost interest in him; I don't care if he lives and I don't care if he dies. But that wouldn't really count as full forgiveness; it's too apathetic a state of mind for that. Forgiveness is a more positive thing: as well as overcoming ill will, the forgiver takes up an attitude of goodwill towards the perpetrator. Forgiving someone involves, to some extent, wishing him well, and this is one of the sources of disquiet about it. Why should we have goodwill towards someone who hasn't shown goodwill to others, who has on the contrary shown them contempt and malice?

Something else we should notice about forgiveness is that in most cases it's something that can't be demanded of the victim, especially not by the perpetrator; he has no right at all to demand forgiveness from his victims. (I might in time come to forgive my dog-killing neighbour, and perhaps I ought to, but it's not for *him* to demand that I do so.) People can perhaps be encouraged by others to forgive, but in most cases they aren't morally *obliged* to forgive someone who's wronged them and, if they choose to do so, it's in the nature of a gift that they give to the offender. It's true that there are some cases where we really ought to forgive a person who has done us wrong: when the wrong wasn't very great, when the perpetrator of it has repented, has apologised and made restitution, and when no harm to others will result from the restoration of goodwill towards the offender. A friend has snapped at you quite unjustifiably when you merely voiced some mild criticisms of her political views. Later she apologises; she is really ashamed of her unfriendly behaviour. Perhaps she offers an excuse: she was feeling unwell, or had had a bad day at work. Or perhaps she doesn't excuse herself; she acknowledges that she was just wrong to be so touchy, and had no business biting your head off like that, especially when you're such a good and long-standing friend. How petty and mean would you have to be to refuse to accept the apology, and refuse to forgive? In cases like that, forgiveness seems to be a duty: it's what we're obliged to do. To say in such cases that we ought to forgive is to say that, all things considered, it's the right thing to do, it's the thing we have most reason to do. And sometimes this is correct.

But cases like that are only a small sector of the rich and diverse range of human wrongdoings, many of which involve appalling and irreparable harm to the primary victim and to others (such as those who love her); and in many of these cases the perpetrator has felt, and still feels, no remorse for his crimes. Think of the rapist who relishes the thought of his own crimes, who when brought to trial insists on conducting his own defence in court, who uses this opportunity to cross-examine the victim in the most humiliating way he can manage, and who clearly revels in her consequent discomfiture and distress at having to redescribe, and hence relive, the traumatic experiences he inflicted on her. Here forgiveness, if it takes place at all, is a completely unforced gift given by the victim to the perpetrator. But why on earth should victims offer offenders that gift? Whatever reasons there are to forgive, to adopt a stance of well-wishing towards the wrongdoers who have caused such harm, how can they be strong enough to outweigh the powerful reasons there are to hate and resent the perpetrator whose only regret about his crimes is that he got caught?

To answer this question, we'll need to look closely at the kinds of considerations that tell against forgiveness. Once again, we'll find it helpful to start with the historical context of our ideas about refusing to forgive.

The historical context

Despite the prevalence of Christianity in Western culture, forgiveness has not always been a dominant value, unquestioningly endorsed. Alongside that religious tradition, and sometimes intermingled with it, there has been another and different code of behaviour: a code of honour and chivalry that requires that insults be avenged, and that regards a stain against honour as more to be feared than wounds and death. That tradition, quite as much as the Christian one, appeals to values and traits that we still find admirable, such as standing up against the aggressor, and scorning an easy life bought at too great a cost to self-respect. The notion of respect, both from others and (crucially) from oneself in the form of self-respect, is central to this array of values, and its presence and influence in the modern world can hardly be overstated, from the gang-members' demands for respect from all comers to the multiculturalist's insistence on respect for all cultures. Although it's sometimes been associated with conservative right-wing political attitudes, as a distinctively aristocratic value, it's also been highly influential on the other side of the political spectrum: the left-wing revolutionary slogan "Better to die on your feet than to live on your knees!" is one expression of this value, one that many people can immediately understand and sympathize with, even where they don't entirely agree with it.

Forgiveness, by contrast, can seem supine, ignoble, feeble and cowardly. It tells us to return good for evil, to show goodwill to those who have harmed us. But some people find this response to wrongdoing simply indistinguishable from a spineless and submissive acceptance of the wrongdoer's low opinion of his victim. Aspects of this contempt for forgiveness can be found in many writers, perhaps most vividly in the works of Nietzsche.

Nietzsche is particularly interested in resentment, the resentment that we have to overcome if we're to forgive those who have harmed us. Who is it, he asks, that experiences resentment? It's tempting to think that absolutely everyone feels this in response to being injured, but in Nietzsche's view it's primarily the weak and powerless who suffer from resentment, whereas the strong (whom he admired) simply do not feel it: they are above such things. And what, asks Nietzsche, is actually going on when the weak overcome resentment and forgive their tormentors? What they're really doing, he proposes, is effectively evading the struggle we all have to participate in, the struggle for recognition by others as being worthy of respect. The weak who forgive are acceding to the perpetrator's lack of respect for them; indeed, they themselves share his low opinion, but they hope to draw its sting by saying that their own needs and rights don't really matter, that what's important is to establish good relations with everyone else, including those who have injured them. In this way they aim to avoid the pain of being dependent – as we all are – on the opinions of others, the pain not only of being the object of hostility or contempt, but also of experiencing the resentment that characteristically produces in us. Most of us try to deal with such pains by fighting back in one way or another, by taking part in the struggle for recognition by others as independent agents. In Nietzsche's view, those who by contrast engage in self-abnegating forgiveness feebly opt out of this struggle, refusing to fight against ill-treatment, and offering love rather than resistance to their enemies. They forgive in order to alleviate their own pain, and disguise this from themselves under the self-admiring rubric of Christian or humanitarian forgiveness.

So Nietzsche in fact shares the therapeutic conception of forgiveness; he thinks that victims forgive their tormentors in order to make themselves feel better. But unlike its modern advocates, Nietzsche holds this kind of therapeutic manoeuvre in contempt. He thinks that far from being an act of generosity, forgiveness in its various manifestations is a self-centred attempt by the victim to salve her own injured vanity: to alleviate the wounds created in her both by the original offence, and by the bitter experience of her resentment of that offence. Where forgiveness is driven by self-abnegating Christian love or any secular version of that, the victim (on Nietzsche's view) denies her own importance, thereby protecting herself from the strain and effort of the struggle for recognition, and from the possibility of incurring further damage in it. Her forgiveness is a way of seeking to become immune to the depredations of others; if you don't engage in a struggle then you can't be injured in it. The forgiver takes refuge in what is ultimately a narcissistic illusion of self-sufficiency.

Nietzsche concludes that in advocating forgiveness, the weak clutch at a delusion, at the fantasy that they can protect themselves from being harmed or despised by others. It is a pretence by the weak that they have the capacities of the strong: that by offering the gift of forgiveness they can somehow remove themselves from the daily struggle to maintain their standing in the eyes of others. He sees the self-abnegating forgiver as a person who "already feels all resisting, all need for resistance, as an unbearable displeasure ... and knows blessedness (pleasure) only in no longer resisting anyone or anything, neither the evil or the evildoer". Far from being admirable, such motivations are, Nietzsche points out, despicable in their narcissism and dishonesty.

What Nietzsche has to tell us is an important part of the argument against forgiveness: if we are to advocate successfully for forgiveness (especially unconditional forgiveness) we need to show that, properly understood, it need not involve any of these contemptible characteristics.

But before that we should take a closer look at three main aspects of the case against forgiveness: the problems with the therapeutic conception; the contrast between revenge and justice; and the significance of respect for the victim.

Problems with the therapeutic conception

First, the current advocacy of forgiveness as a form of therapy can be deeply objectionable to victims. Consider the women victims of the civil wars that have raged in Sudan and the Congo: tens of thousands of women have been tortured and raped by combatants as deliberate acts of war. (Such things also took place in Europe in the wars of the Yugoslav succession in the 1990s, and of course extensively during the Second World War.) According to the United Nations, approximately 200,000 women have been raped in the Congo during the past twelve years. These rapes are often accompanied by sadistic mutilating violence of exceptional ferocity. People who have suffered such terrible wrongs, and who bear a heavy load of justifiable resentment and hostility towards their tormentors, may find the widespread advocacy of forgiveness as a therapeutic device unbearably glib and facile. Even those who aren't themselves victims can see how superficial this advocacy often is. It amounts to what has been called "cheap boosterism" about forgiveness: the pretence that it's a ready solution to the ills produced by wrongdoing, that it's easily available to all who want to cure those ills, and also that it's morally unassailable, that there are no moral reasons against it, in all circumstances. To victims labouring under the burden of an entirely warranted resentment and outrage, this account of what is supposed to be the right course of action for them can immediately delegitimize their genuine and justified hostility to those who have done them unspeakable harm. Constant public praise of forgiveness, and the easy assumption that forgiving is always the best thing to do, may leave victims with no acceptable way of expressing the rage and contempt that they may actually and legitimately feel. In these circumstances, the generous endorsement of forgiveness for the perpetrators is made at the expense of the victims, whose actual responses to the violations that have been done to them remain unvalidated, and sometimes even unheard.

Even those of us who have never suffered the terrible moral barbarities that wars typically produce may nonetheless have had serious offences committed against us. (Having lesser offences committed against us is of course the common human condition, as is committing lesser offences against others; this is why we all have an interest in forgiveness). Think of a parent whose child is systematically, relentlessly, bullied by another child, and also by the bully's adult relatives and friends, who gather together day after day to mock and jeer and sneer at and humiliate their miserable victim. (Sometimes children who have to suffer such bullying kill them-

29

selves.) The mother of that poor child, who may be effectively help-less to prevent the bullying, may well feel that forgiving her child's tormentors would be a way of making light of the child's misery, and that people who so cheerfully recommend forgiveness to her have simply failed, or refused, to see her child's misery and predicament for what it really is: a form of dreadful persecution. Telling her to focus on wishing the persecutors well can seem not only misplaced advice but a positive distortion of morality. In one recent tragic case, a mother killed herself and her disabled daughter after ten years of bullying and harassment by gangs of local children, and many failed attempts to get the police to intervene. Would advising that mother to forgive have been a morally acceptable response to her terrible predicament?

The therapeutic conception of forgiveness assumes that forgive-ness is what's needed to free the victim from her suffering, and that any other attitude is therapeutically ineffective and morally inad-equate. But this simply isn't true: there's plenty of reason to believe that forgiveness isn't the only way of overcoming the trauma of victimhood. Revenge will sometimes do the business: it's a mistake to assume that revenge is always a disappointment to the one who exacts it. Sometimes revenge does deliver the satisfaction it prom-ises. Victims who take revenge can sometimes feel freed there-after of the wrongs that have been done to them; they sometimes achieve closure, and feel that justice and some kind of equity has been restored to their lives. Although there are many things that are wrong, morally and pragmatically, with revenge, it's a specious illusion to suppose that it never provides a psychological resolution of the bitterness and resentment that victims have to suffer.

So even if forgiveness is as therapeutic as is sometimes claimed, it's not the only form of therapy available for the victims of wrong-doing. Think of *Hamlet*, where the whole play turns on the Prince's inability to take decisive revenge on the murderer of his father, and the torment this indecisiveness causes him. (The fact that

Shakespeare's play is one of a more general dramatic type called "revenge tragedies" is some indication of how significant revenge has always seemed to us.) Think also of the moral code implicit in the Western film genre, where resisting, and punishing, and often taking explicit revenge on, whoever are currently the villains is absolutely central to so many of the plots. Revenge is a very satisfying part of that whole fictional world, and also of the real world it (to some extent) mimics. So if we're just thinking of what makes people feel good after they've been wronged, revenge has to be a serious candidate alongside forgiveness. We can't allow the fact that we might prefer forgiveness as a more moral alternative to blind us to the possibility that revenge may sometimes be quite as therapeutically effective.

However, critics of the therapeutic case for forgiveness needn't believe or imply that revenge is the only satisfactory alternative to it. Victims who refuse to forgive offenders may be gripped by a desire not for vengeance but for justice; and in maintaining resentment they may be insisting that we should not lose our morally essential sense of the responsibility and the culpability of those who have committed terrible wrongs. This may be particularly important at the social level: after terrible social conflicts, with all their attendant atrocities, the persistence of resentment among the victims may be what's needed to protect us all from the easy forgetfulness that would allow the horrors of the past to be recreated in the future. What a broken society needs may be justice rather than (or at least prior to) forgiveness, since without justice the embers of conflict may well at some point burst into flame again. Unless perpetrators are publicly brought to justice and punished for their misdeeds, we're unlikely, so this argument goes, to be able to prevent future atrocities of the same or worse kind from taking place. The suggestion here is that for social stability justice is at least as therapeutically important as forgiveness.

Justice and revenge

But in any case, there are arguments against forgiveness that go well beyond the therapeutic conception or the problems that it raises. Some, perhaps much, of the pressure on victims to forgive implies that those who refuse to do so are morally defective: perhaps understandably, considering what has been done to them, but nonetheless (it is implied) in a condition that is morally inferior to that of the generously forgiving person. On this picture, all the *moral* considerations are seen as weighing in on the side of forgiveness, whereas what count against forgiveness are thought to be more primitive and emotional reasons, such as the desire for revenge. But as it stands, this picture just begs the question against the possibility of a morally serious maintenance of resentment; it simply *assumes* that it's immoral to refuse to forgive. But that's the very thing that needs to be justified: we need to be given the *reasons* for thinking that morality is entirely on the side of forgiveness.

Contrary to that pro-forgiveness picture, there may in fact be very serious moral reasons for maintaining resentment and other hostile attitudes towards the perpetrator. Even if it's true that forgiveness releases the victim from psychological bondage to the past and enables her to take up more positive attitudes, this isn't the only important consideration. Victims needn't, and in fact often don't, put their own mental well-being first in these matters. For some, at least, the demand for justice takes priority. Victims who have this attitude may not be primarily concerned with their own healing or well-being at all; their demand for justice or retribution may come from an overwhelming duty which they feel towards those who died as a result of the perpetrators' crimes. Or they may see the demand for justice as morally compelling in its own right, as necessary to remedy a violation of the moral order, quite irrespective of its effects on their psyches. A survivor of atrocities who insists that recognizing and acknowledging breaches of the moral order is more important than questions of her own psychological health is not adopting a morally negligible position. Victims who take this attitude towards wrongdoers may well be sacrificing their own well-being, not for the sake of revenge, but in the name of a higher sense of justice.

It's a profound mistake to think that demands for justice that are driven by indignation at the offender's breach of the moral order are equivalent to demands for revenge. Justice has various important aspects, including the aim of deterring future wrongdoers from committing offences; but a central element in most people's conception of criminal justice, at any rate, is that of retribution, of inflicting a punishment on the offender because he *deserves* it (and *only* because he deserves it). It's true that revenge normally shares this concern for punishing the perpetrator. But although revenge and justice overlap in this and other areas, they also differ in many morally important ways. Revenge is private and personal; it relishes the suffering it inflicts on its object; it readily (although by no means invariably) aims for disproportionate punishment of the offender. Justice by contrast is public; it's constrained by considerations to do with even-handedness, fairness and desert; enjoyment of the suffering produced in the offender is no part of it. It's a profoundly moral concept: if we have to choose between justice and forgiveness, then we're choosing between differing moral considerations, rather than between morality and some more self-interested or discreditable reason for action such as the desire for unalloyed revenge.

But at this point some people may feel that we're overlooking a genuine and deep connection between justice and revenge, one that makes them morally more similar than we've acknowledged here. The connection lies in the role played by punishment in both of them: justice for serious offences will normally require punishment, and since punishment involves some degree of suffering, then justice, it may be argued, also seeks suffering for its own sake, so it can't after all be distinguished from revenge in this centrally important respect.

However, this too is a mistake. Revenge is usually a response to wrongful action (although this isn't always the case – people sometimes take revenge for actions by others they just greatly dislike, even where those actions aren't in any way wrong), but nonetheless the focus of revenge isn't on rectifying that wrong. Revenge isn't primarily concerned with the restoration of the moral order. Rather, what the vengeful person seeks is the satisfaction of seeing the perpetrator suffer, whether or not that suffering serves justice. In contrast to this, rectifying the wrong and restoring the moral order is the centrally important thing for retributive justice. No satisfaction is taken in the suffering of the perpetrator for its own sake, but only in so far as it serves justice. (In fact, if those who impose justice on wrongdoers do seem to be taking pleasure in the suffering involved then we begin to think that justice isn't what they're primarily concerned with.) The attitudes of the vengeful person to the suffering imposed in just punishment are usually noticeably different from the attitudes of the person whose moral indignation makes them seek justice for the victim. The person who is justly indignant, but not vengeful, will be pleased if the offender's punishment may rightfully be lessened, perhaps because the offender repents and reforms, or because it's discovered that the offence was less severe than was originally thought to be the case, or it was mitigated or excused in some way. In so far as the justly indignant person seeks the offender's suffering, she doesn't desire it for its own sake, but only because it's an ineliminable element in punishment, and punishment is necessary to redress the wrong that has been committed. The vengeful person, by contrast, will gloat over the downfall and even the degradation of the one who has wronged him, and will be frustrated if it turns out that the wrongdoer deserves a lesser punishment than the vengeful person would find satisfying. (Many of us have at some point experienced, to our shame, a faint but genuine sense of disappointment when the evidence shows that people whom we really disapprove of aren't in fact quite as wicked as we've believed them to be.) Demands for retributive justice really aren't equivalent to demands for revenge, and the victim whose sustained resentment is a way of maintaining the demand for justice isn't morally equivalent to one who purely seeks revenge for wrongs which have been done to her.

The relations between justice and vengeance are complex, as we can see in an illuminating story told by Jared Diamond:

> Jozef … passed up the opportunity for vengeance and lived to regret it. Jozef was a Polish Jew who was captured by the Soviets in 1939 and sent to a Siberian camp before becoming an officer in a Polish division of the Red Army. In the summer of 1945, he led an armed platoon to Klaj, Poland, to discover what had happened to his mother, his sister, and his niece. There he learned that an armed gang had shot them, but when he was face-to-face with the man who led the gang, he hesitated to shoot. Instead, he delivered him to the police, who investigated the crime and then, after about a year, released the murderer. Until his death, Jozef remained tormented by regret at his failure to take vengeance.   (Diamond 2008)

Here the victim, the soldier whose family has been murdered, actually prefers justice to vengeance, and only when justice is effectively denied him does he regret the lost opportunity to take vengeance instead. It looks as if vengeance is a *substitute* for justice for this victim, rather than an equivalent; what drives his desire for vengeance is the knowledge that justice for him and for his dead family has been denied. In this case, far from justice being merely a mask for vengeance, it's an independent consideration of the first moral importance, one that, if it can be attained, is actually preferable to revenge.

35

Respect for the victim

We have good reasons to provide justice, with its attendant publicity and punishment, for the sake of the victims, dead or alive. It's something that people care very deeply about when they've been adversely treated, and it's appropriate in itself, since it's what the perpetrators deserve. So if we emphasize only the good that forgiveness without justice will do, for the individual victim or for the society that has been riven by conflict, then we're effectively demanding that considerations of justice should be subordinated to considerations of future personal or social flourishing. But in doing this we do seem to be treating the victims as if they, and their sufferings, weren't in the end of any great moral significance. And this is one of the major arguments against forgiveness: in readily forgiving the offender, it is said, we fail to show sufficient respect for the victim. Where the offence is at the individual level, the victim's readiness to forgive the offender shows, according to this argument, a failure in self-respect. Every offence displays at the very least a neglect of the importance of the victim, a refusal to recognize her status as someone who should be treated with respect, and hence someone who should be neither attacked nor exploited. And a victim who is ready to forgive an offender who has failed to show her this fundamental respect is, on the view we're considering here, colluding with the offender's low estimation of her status. Rather than being large-minded and generous, she is, on this view (which is closely related to Nietzsche's critique of forgiveness) being submissively deferential to one who effectively despises her, and this involves her in an unlovely and unjustified failure of self-respect.

Where forgiveness is called for at the societal level, perhaps after some murderous social conflict, then there is a question about who it is that should do the forgiving. Very often it can't be the principal victims, since they are dead. So forgiveness may be looked for from victims' families, and other members of their ethnic or religious groups, as well as from those victims who have survived. In this case a similar objection is often raised: too easy a forgiveness fails to respect those who have suffered from the perpetrators' wrongdoing. Ready forgiveness of the offender, acceptance of him back into the circle of goodwill for the sake of the benefit to the rest of society, doesn't seem to provide adequate respect for his victims. A major way of showing people respect is providing justice to them when they've been wrongly treated. If, for the sake of future peace and social stability, we choose to provide forgiveness to the perpetrator rather than justice for the victim, then we're trading off the justice and respect that we owe to victims against future social good – that is, the good of others. Even where we think there is good reason to do this, we shouldn't deny that there is a price to be paid: the victims (or their families) will be denied justice for the sake of the general good, and to that extent they're being treated with less respect than they deserve.

Closely allied to these concerns about insufficient respect is another criticism of forgiveness, one that claims that in being so ready to offer forgiveness we often fail to grasp the full weight and gravity of what the offender did. But it is that very moral weight that justifies the victim in responding with hostility and resentment. If a perpetrator has harmed a victim, and dismissed her needs and interests as of no concern, then this is a serious matter. The victim is *justified* in resenting it, and it's reasonable for her to withdraw goodwill from such a person. A person who fully grasps the nature of the offence and what it has done to the victim will respond with indignation at the very least, and often with ill will. This ill will is what is overcome in forgiveness, and too ready a forgiveness suggests that there wasn't much hostility to struggle with, which in turn suggests that the full weight of the offence hasn't really been grasped, since, if it had, the natural response to it would have cost some effort to overcome.

This objection to forgiveness rests on the background view that emotions and beliefs aren't fully separate: that if you have certain beliefs, then you'll have the emotions that go with those beliefs too. Someone who properly grasps the nature of an atrocity, say, will naturally have the appropriate feelings of horror and disgust; and if he doesn't, that gives us reason to think that he hasn't fully understood what's going on. On a smaller scale and closer to home, think of the last time you did something that really shames you, something really mean or petty or thoroughly selfish. How do you feel about it? Probably you feel anger and self-disgust (we all have this experience, although most of us are quite good at hiding it from others, and sometimes even from ourselves.) If you don't have these feelings, it's quite likely that you don't really believe that what you did was genuinely mean or petty or thoroughly selfish. In fact, if someone says that she knows she's been spiteful and self-centred, but seems to feel no distress at this, seems to be emotionally quite calm and satisfied with herself, we're likely to conclude that she doesn't really believe that her behaviour was bad. Here, as elsewhere, affective and cognitive responses are not fully separable: if we have certain kinds of belief then we'll have the relevant emotions too. The person who feels too little indignation at the spectacle of serious wrong-doing is suffering from both an emotional and a cognitive deficit: he lacks both a full understanding of the wrong and also the right feelings about it. Where resentment is minimal because indignation is minimal, forgiveness comes cheap; but it's bought at the expense of a failure to recognize and respond appropriately to the true gravity of the offence. Here the argument against forgiveness is an argument that a proper sense of how serious the offence was will rightly result in a degree of indignation and resentment that will be hard to overcome. Anyone who forgives easily will thereby show that he hasn't properly grasped the moral weight of the offence and of the perpetrator's culpability for it. It's more important, according to this argument, that we should understand the real nature of wrongdoing, and consequently experience the appropriate reactions to it of anger and resentment, than that we should gloss over that moral seriousness, allow ourselves to be blind to it, for the sake of a cheap resolution of moral conflict in a facile forgiveness.

These considerations are bolstered by the patently obvious fact that sometimes forgiveness is motivated by considerations that are morally fairly dubious. People may offer forgiveness in order to demonstrate their moral superiority, or to put others at a moral disadvantage, or to curry favour with powerful offenders or with people who approve of forgiveness, or to heap a burden of guilt on the shoulders of the offender or on the shoulders of other less-forgiving bystanders. There can be a multiplicity of bad motives for doing good things, and forgiveness is no different from other actions in this respect.

So where have we got to in the case against forgiveness? The principal arguments against forgiveness claim that:

- It doesn't always have the therapeutic effects claimed for it, either at the individual or at the societal level.
- Forgiveness is not the only route to achieving these therapeutic effects.
- In some cases at least forgiveness is actually damaging, both at the individual and at the societal level.
- Even if it does have strongly therapeutic effects, that alone doesn't settle the moral argument, since other things may sometimes be more important than therapeutic considerations.
- One of these things is justice, which is morally important in its own right, and may in some circumstances produce better outcomes than forgiveness.
- Forgiveness often involves too little respect for the victim as a person.
- Forgiveness often involves a failure to grasp the nature and extent of the offence against the victim.

- Forgiveness can be, and often is, motivated by craven or self-serving considerations, which have no claim on our moral attention.

The case against forgiveness, especially against unconditional forgiveness – forgiveness of offenders who haven't repented of their crimes – is a formidable one. It is also in many ways a morally satisfying one: quite as satisfying, in its different way, as is the case in favour of forgiveness. Where the case for forgiveness speaks to our desire for reconciliation, harmony and generosity, the case against it satisfies our commitment to justice, to moral responsibility, to an uncompromising rejection of atrocity. It legitimizes our desire to bear witness to the iniquity of what has been done to the innocent, and to make explicit our refusal to collude with those crimes in any way.

It is true that the case against forgiveness can be abused and exploited in various ways. People can sternly refuse to forgive, and bitterly discourage others from forgiving, for reasons they claim are to do with justice and responsibility, when really what is motivating them is a very powerful (and discreditable) pleasure in blaming others and inflicting punishment on them. The desire to blame others, and to dwell on and make much of their shortcomings and vices, is one that can be found in all times and places; it's a human constant, and a very unlovely one. It's very often found both in the popular press and also in the quality press; education and knowledge are no barrier against it. Most of us can feel some poisonous shreds of it in our own natures. This rancorous and mean-spirited exposure and enjoyment of the moral weakness of others can easily masquerade as a proper concern to uphold justice and ensure that people get what they deserve. But the fact that the case against forgiveness can be abused doesn't in any way show that it should be dismissed. The case in *favour* of forgiveness can also be abused: cheap boosterism about forgiveness can exploit our desire to seem generous, sympathetic, morally elevated; to embrace a hoped-for rosy future and to forget about the ugly and sometimes horrifying past, and about the inconvenient and often quite costly demands for justice from those who suffered in that past. Praise for forgiveness of those who have harmed others can readily slide into a light-minded dismissal of the weight and gravity of those harms. We can't judge the case for *or* the case against forgiveness by its vulnerability to abuse, since that exists so prominently on both sides. Here, as elsewhere, we can only assess each case on the basis of its actual strengths and weaknesses.

Although the case against forgiveness is indeed a strong one, it isn't necessarily conclusive. Some, at least, of its objections to forgiveness can be met, and others can be defused by careful analysis of what is at issue. That's what we'll look at in Chapter 5. But first, we must consider whether a different response is possible: a third way, neither hatred nor forgiveness, which perhaps can avoid the problems on either side. That will be the subject matter of Chapter 3.

3. A third way?

Esther Mujawayo lost hundreds of relatives, including her mother, her father, and her husband, in conditions of unspeakable brutality and horror during the Rwandan genocide of 1994. In her writings after the end of the massacres she wrote:

"I don't want to understand [the killers], at least, not yet. I want to proceed step by step: within ten years maybe. I don't want to understand ... I say to myself that some people are paid for that, for understanding the killers – politicians, humanitarian staff, right-thinking people ... all those whose work is to get into contact with criminals. Myself, I don't need that. I don't want to understand them and I don't want to excuse them. They did it ... and I want them to pay for that and not to sleep soundly. ...

All those I met in Rwanda, until the survivors working on the field, ... never think about forgiveness .... However, all of them work in favour of a reconciliation. Because to reconcile does not mean to forgive. To take up with neighbours again, starting with the ability to greet each other, is important for all the reasons that I have already emphasized: our culture cannot be conceived without these traditions, these rituals."

(Quoted in Brudholm & Rosoux 2009: 33)

The need for forgiveness (if forgiveness is in fact what's needed) arises out of human conflict. The perpetrator's wrongdoing is the locus of that conflict; it may indeed have started it, and it has to be handled in some way or other by the victim. An offence that is at all serious isn't the kind of thing that can readily be overlooked or completely ignored; and even if the victim does in the end decide to overlook or ignore it, that itself is a choice about how to handle the conflict, and there are other choices that can be made. In some situations the perpetrator's power is so great that he can simply impose his will on his victims without their having any redress at all, but still the victim has to choose what attitude to adopt, and different people do this differently. In circumstances where the victim is completely in her oppressor's power, so that it may be literally fatal for her to overtly express any attitude but complete obedience and deference to the perpetrator, there still can be inner differences in response to such oppression. In the demonic world of the Nazi concentration camps, some were totally crushed by the horrors in which they were immersed, and lost the capacity to make any autonomous responses at all; others retained this, and were able to varying extents to reflect on and judge their tormentors; still others – a very few – were able to plan and sometimes execute some form of resistance. Such people did not of course live very long. Primo Levi, a survivor and a witness of remarkable moral clarity and judgement, said that those who survived knew that the best had all died. (In any case, inmates in the camps, however they responded to the horror of their circumstances, rarely lived for longer than a few months.) Perhaps it is misleading to talk of *choice* of response in such extreme circumstances, and certainly it's not for us to imply any criticism of those who had to undergo such horrors. But even in the depths of those hells victims responded in different ways to the nightmare conditions that the perpetrators produced.

Certainly in less extreme circumstances the victim has to decide how to behave in response to the offence and its aftermath. In relatively small-scale offences in private life, involving personal hostilities or betrayals, the victim can, if she wants to, choose to cut off

43

all further contact with the offender; but in cases of widespread conflict where a whole society has been involved this option may simply not be available. If normal life is ever to be resumed, there has to be some kind of resolution of the conflict, one way or another. Forgiveness provides one such resolution, but there are many others. Maintaining resentment and anger, and insisting on punishment, is another one, and that's often a very attractive resolution in the eyes of the victim and those close to her. But anger and punishment don't always yield the psychological satisfaction expected of them. Victims sometimes find that they don't get the closure they hoped for: not from revenge, and not from justice either. And although the procedures of justice – the trial, with the public presentation of evidence about the wrongdoing, and the later sentencing and punishment – are often of the first importance in creating and maintaining social order, there are times when this isn't the case. Where the community has been deeply divided by violent conflict along religious or ethnic or ideological grounds, then the mechanisms of retributive justice aren't always the best way to reduce the likelihood of conflict breaking out again (although sometimes they are: we shouldn't underestimate the deterrent power of swift and severe punishment).

The demands of justice may require that the perpetrator be punished, in which case that punishment can be justified independently of whether it produces good consequences for either the victim or the wider social community. For as we saw in Chapter 2, their good isn't always the most important thing, and sometimes sustained anger and outrage, and retributive punishment, just do seem to be what the offence itself calls for. Perhaps it's something we owe to the dead victims, irrespective of whether it helps to prevent future conflicts or produce other good outcomes. Nonetheless, the need to resolve conflict and diminish the chances of its resurgence are important matters that mustn't be overlooked. There are circumstances in which the punishment of those who have committed atrocious crimes, deeply deserved though it would be, may not produce a socially bearable outcome. It's not uncommon for perpetrators who see that they may be going to lose power to strike a bargain with those who will replace them, in which they give up their power with less struggle, and hence less bloodshed for their victims, in return for promises of immunity for their crimes. Unjust though such bargains certainly are, they may involve the saving of so many lives that they can't be dismissed out of hand as hopelessly immoral. The lives of future victims are no less important than the lives of past ones (although no more important either, of course.)

In fact it may not always be possible to punish wrongdoers; after the horrors of civil war, for example, it may simply be beyond the capacity of a country's justice system to provide fair trials and appropriate punishment for all who committed war crimes. Ten years after the genocide in Rwanda, in which approximately 800,000 people were killed in the course of three months, the jails in that country still contained around 80,000 people accused of crimes connected with those terrible killings. The United Nations International Criminal Tribunal for Rwanda had managed to convict ten detainees in approximately ten years, at a cost of hundreds of millions of dollars. The Rwandan courts, which were also bringing detainees to trial, had nothing like the UN Tribunal budget, and in any case couldn't cope with the huge numbers involved. There was no realistic prospect of bringing the genocidaires to justice. Whatever was going to bring a resolution to the aftermath of that hideous conflict, and prevent it breaking out again, it wasn't going to be due process and just punishment.

And of course not all wrongdoings are appropriately met with punishment, since not all of them involve crimes. If a close friend deceives and betrays us he may have committed a profound wrong, but if he's broken no law, then the question of punishment may not really come up. But even in those cases where punishment has been appropriate and has taken place, the question still arises:

what now? What attitude to the offender should the victim adopt? Forgiveness is one answer, but it isn't always an easy thing to do; there are many reasons against forgiving perpetrators; and as we have seen the victim's motives for forgiveness may sometimes be so morally dubious that it isn't clear that forgiveness of *that* kind is really what we ought to do at all.

Before we consider whether forgiveness can be rescued from these and other criticisms, we need to investigate the possibility that there may be other and better ways of dealing with the aftermath of wrongdoing. Is forgiveness the only alternative to permanent hatred and resentment, with all the moral and psychological problems that raises? Or are there other ways of dealing with wrongdoing that don't involve the maintenance of hatred, but don't require full-blown forgiveness either? Perhaps there is a third way, neither hatred nor forgiveness, which has more to commend it than either of these.

What exactly would we want of such a third way – what do we look for when we aim to devise the best way to deal with wrong-doing and the aftermath of conflict? If we try to construct a check-list of the features we'd hope to find it might look something like this:

- it should acknowledge the truth of what happened to the victim;
- at the very least, it should do no further harm to surviving victims, and should not press them to respond in ways they find unacceptable;
- it should give proper weight to the victims' demands for justice;
- if possible it should lift the burden of victimhood off their shoulders, leaving them able to move on from the offence without permanent psychological damage;
- however, it should also recognize that "moving on" is sometimes morally inappropriate, and that resistance to this needn't be either psychologically or morally pathological;

- it should promote the resolution of conflict and enable the parties to previous conflict to live together, at least where they wish to;
- it should also make life together bearable in cases where separation simply isn't possible, as in the aftermath of national conflict;
- and finally, it should be not only morally permissible but also morally desirable – we want to know what is the *right* thing for us to do, the right attitude to take, to our erstwhile (and sometimes present) adversaries.

If we could find a response to wrongdoing that met all these requirements, that would be a tremendous strike in favour of it: we'd have really good reason to endorse it. We'll consider three main possibilities for a response to conflict that amounts neither to hatred nor to forgiveness: first, seeking to understand the causes of the wrongdoing; second, rising above the offence; third, political reconciliation. We can then see how they measure up to the checklist we've created above.

1. Understanding the causes

One possible response to wrongdoing is to seek understanding of it, in the hope that this will resolve the conflict it has created. The proponents of this view sometimes quote the French proverb, "To understand all is to forgive all". This is one of these very attractive sayings that nonetheless cries out for further explanation: *why* will we forgive everything if we understand everything? How is this supposed to work?

Various different ideas seem to be packed into this superficially uncontentious and blameless thought. One is the suggestion that if we see why the perpetrator wanted to commit his offence, we'll see why he saw it as a good thing to do, and so we'll no longer regard him as alien, as different from us, and to be rejected and condemned. Another closely connected idea is that if we understand the root causes of the wrongdoer's actions we'll come to see that we too, if we'd been acted on by those causes, would have done what he did, and hence we won't want to blame him for his actions. "There but for the grace of God go I", people sometimes say, meaning that if we had been in the wrongdoer's position, we too would have done what he did, and hence we shouldn't blame him. A further, and stronger, way of thinking about the search for the root causes of wrongdoing is to see them as revealing that the wrongdoer wasn't actually to blame at all: it's not just that we won't *want* to blame him, it's that there really will be nothing to blame him for, because given those causes he couldn't have done anything other than what he did. This view amounts to saying that once the causes of his action were in place, the offender couldn't have acted differently, and so there are no grounds for attributing blame.

So there are different elements in this proposal about the need for understanding and its value for resolving conflict, but they have one thing in common: they all amount to the claim that understanding will remove blame, and this will help to produce a resolution of the conflict created by the offence. But they also have another thing in common: although they look like morally attractive ideas (who wants to object to greater understanding, after all?) they're all deeply unsatisfactory as a response to genuine wrongdoing, and the worse the wrongdoing is, the more objectionable is this kind of response.

There is, of course, nothing wrong with increasing our understanding; that's not what's objectionable about this approach to wrongdoing. The problem lies in what are supposed to be the implications for blame and responsibility. Take the first idea: that understanding leads to forgiveness because we come to see why the wrongdoer thought that what he was doing was good, and so we no longer want to blame him for his actions. Although the talk here is of forgiveness, what's really going on isn't forgiveness but *excuse*: we think the offender isn't to be blamed, because he mistakenly thought that what he was doing was good. The mugger thought that the only way for him to get respect from his peers was to steal the material goods that he didn't himself possess from a stranger on the street; he's wrong about this, and indeed about the value of that kind of respect, but we can understand the difficulties he faced, and why he thought, and hence acted, the way he did. But this is a proffered *excuse*. To excuse someone is to say that he isn't really to blame for the offence, and hence that anger and resentment are misplaced. Forgiveness is quite different from that: what it says is that the offender really is to blame for the offence, and hence anger and resentment are perfectly reasonable reactions to him; but nonetheless the forgiver is going to forego hostile attitudes and look on the perpetrator with goodwill. That's part of what makes forgiveness so difficult: it recognizes that the offender truly is to blame, but still offers him a well-wishing attitude. Excuses, in contrast, deny that the offender is to blame at all.

Now sometimes excuses are genuinely called-for, and if our best understanding of the wrongdoer shows that he really isn't to blame, and hence ought to be excused, then that's what we should do. But we can't suppose that understanding *always* leads to excusing. In fact we know very intimately that it doesn't and shouldn't: consider what happens when we come, perhaps by reflection on our own behaviour, or perhaps through the honest remarks of others, to understand our own less appealing motives. Sometimes this involves understanding that we've acted out of selfishness, or vindictiveness, or craven cowardice; that, for example, our real motive for criticizing our colleagues wasn't to pursue the truth in a spirit of impersonal enquiry, but rather to do others down and to show ourselves in a better light. Here we come to understand that envy and spite play more of a role in our behaviour than we're at all happy to believe of ourselves. Such increases in self-understanding are common: every adult who hasn't adopted a policy of determinedly excusing everything she does has experienced them. (And even people who have adopted that policy often silently admit to themselves that their motives are sometimes pretty grubby, even if they refuse to acknowledge it to others.) There are dark places in the human psyche, and part of maturing into adulthood is the unwelcome recognition of these things in our own familiar selves. These increases in self-understanding lead us to blame ourselves more rather than less, and although of course we may sometimes be wrong about our own culpability, it takes a very determined optimist about human nature to assert that we're never right to hold ourselves to blame. And if greater understanding of our own dark motives can sometimes rightly lead to greater self-blame, then we have to accept that greater understanding of others will sometimes rightly lead to greater blame of them too.

Look now at the second idea packed into the thought that understanding the offender will resolve our conflict with him: the idea that "There but for the grace of God go I." This claim – that for many of us, if we'd been in the same situation as the offender, we too would have committed a like or even worse offence – is often perfectly true. When we think, for example, of those who in the face of the mass killings of their neighbours stood by silently, neither helping nor hindering the killers, we sometimes realize with horror that we too, in those circumstances, might have done the same thing. But how is this realization supposed to improve the situation created by wrongdoing? The suggestion seems to be that if the offender did what the rest of us, or at least many of the rest of us, would also have done in his shoes, then we're not in a position to blame him; and in the absence of blame there's no further conflict to be resolved. But this suggestion is just hopelessly implausible. Why does my recognition that I too might have done what the offender did imply that I shouldn't blame him? It only has that implication if

I also think that anything *I* do shouldn't ever be blamed, and how much of an egoist do you have to be to really believe that? Surely it's perfectly possible, and much more appropriate, for me to think that I too might have stood by without protesting when others were taken off for torture and death, *and* to think that if I had done so I would have been profoundly to blame.

Perhaps we're supposed to interpret the saying "There but for the grace of God go I" as implying that what the offender did was so much like what anyone would have done in his shoes that we can't really regard it as wrong. The background thought here seems to be that if there's a way of behaving that everyone, or nearly everyone, would adopt, then it's pointless to regard it as really wrong. It's just part of human nature: it's the way we are. We're bound to act like that, given human nature, and there's no point in bewailing the inevitable. But this interpretation is even worse than the last one. First, the fact (if it is a fact) that a way of behaving is part of human nature doesn't mean it's irremediable; think how much natural human aggression, or natural sexual activity, is shaped and constrained by social forces and personal choices. These are certainly natural drives, but how they're expressed can show quite dramatic variations. Second, if the (supposed) fact that we'd all act like that means that what the offender did shouldn't even be regarded as wrong, then that amounts to *condoning* his actions. On either interpretation of "There but for the grace of God go I," it's hard to see how this is going to provide a satisfactory way of dealing with the aftermath of wrongdoing, especially when the effect on the victims of wrongdoing is considered. What we'd be saying, on this approach, would either be that no one is really to blame for the victims' injuries, or alternatively that what was done to them doesn't even really amount to wrongdoing. In spite of the superficially generous motives that may be in play when we say "There but for the grace of God go I", a greater denial of the moral nature of what was done to the victims is hard to imagine.

Even deeper problems arise when we consider the third idea packed into the demand for understanding: the idea that if we know the root causes of the offender's actions, we'll see that he couldn't have acted any differently, and hence there is no scope for blame. This is once again an excuse, but on a very grand scale: the idea here is that our actions are caused, and we're helpless in the face of those causal forces, and hence can't be morally responsible for what we do.

This view at once raises the enormous philosophical problem of free will, a problem too big for us to address properly here. But it's worth looking at the implications of this view: that given the root causes of the offender's actions, he couldn't have done other than what he did – he wasn't free to choose to avoid his wrongdoing. If we only believe this of offenders, we are in effect saying that they're less human than the rest of us, since normally human beings can freely (although within limits) choose how they act; they're not simply the creatures of their circumstances. But thinking of wrong-doers as less human than the rest of us doesn't seem like a promising way of resolving conflict with them.

Alternatively, if we think that this view is true of everyone, wrong-doers and victims alike, so that all of us are the puppets of the causal forces bearing down on us, and none of us can choose how we act, then just consider how much of our ordinary way of thinking about our fellows will have to be abandoned. We won't be able to blame them, true, but we also won't be able to praise them either. If they're not responsible for what they do, then they can't be praised for their heroism or generosity or kindness or fairness, since they couldn't, on this view, help acting in any of these ways. As a consequence we won't be able to maintain a huge range of attitudes to our fellows that are inextricably interwoven with everyday life, attitudes such as resentment, respect, disapproval, admiration. All of these attitudes imply responsibility, and would have to be abandoned if we really believed that people's actions were just the outcome of intersecting causal forces, so that they couldn't be held responsible for them, or be regarded as culpable where they acted wrongly. Our lives, and our relationships with others, would be unrecognizably different and impoverished. And the consequent hollowing out of morality itself would leave us with no way of morally condemning the most terrible atrocities, since they would all merely be the result of their root causes, whatever these turned out to be, and their perpetrators would have been as helplessly at the mercy of those causal forces as the victims themselves.

This conflation of the moral standing of the perpetrators with that of the victims is one of the most unattractive features of any approach to the aftermath of conflict that involves removing blame in general from the wrongdoers. Excusing and condoning wrong-doing won't meet the requirements of our checklist, and in partic-ular are liable to do further harm to the victim, by denying the nature of what was done to her, and effectively declaring a moral equivalence between victim and wrongdoer.

Understanding is a good thing, and the aim of increasing our understanding of wrongdoing is always a legitimate one. For a start, it may help us to prevent wrongdoing from recurring. There may also be individual occasions in which our understanding of the wrongdoer shows us that there is an excuse for him, in which case we can and should withhold blame. But as a general thing, under-standing why perpetrators do wrong needn't by itself show that they're not to blame for what they do. Consider what one of the Rwandan genocidaires, Jean Girumuhatse, later said about his own behaviour during the genocide:

> For me, it became a pleasure to kill. The first time, it's to please the government. After that, I developed a taste for it. I hunted and caught and killed with real enthusiasm. It wasn't like working for the government, it was like working for myself .... I was very, very excited when I killed. I remember each

killing. Yes, I woke every morning excited to go into the bush. It was the hunt-the-human hunt .... The genocide was like a festival. At day's end, or any time there was an occasion, we took a cow from the Tutsis, and slaughtered it and grilled it and drank beer. There were no limits any more. It was a festival. We celebrated.

The journalist who interviewed Girumuhatse commented:

So Girumuhatse had found his vocation as a murderer. Before that, he had been a peasant, as he was again now, tending the fields for beer money and enough beans and bananas to sustain himself, his wife, and seven children. But for a few months in 1994 Rwanda had become a kingdom of death and he had lived more fully, more like a lord, than he had ever imagined possible.   (Gourevitch 2009)

Both the killer's own words, and the interviewer's comments on them, increase our understanding of why this man committed such atrocities. But they don't, and shouldn't, incline us to suppose that he wasn't responsible, or culpable, for what he did. To imply that perpetrators aren't really to blame, and maybe aren't even doing wrong, is to excuse or condone what they do, and thereby to undermine our attempts, weak and insufficient as they already are, to prevent such horrors from happening again. Yoking together understanding and excusing damages the former and turns the latter into a get-out-of-jail-free card for wrongdoers and their sympathisers. If forgiveness is an unsatisfactory response to wrongdoing because it (supposedly) fails to fully acknowledge the importance of the wrong done to the victim, then how much more objectionable and damaging, both to the victim and to the body politic, is a policy of generalized excuse and condoning. We shouldn't, and needn't, allow understanding to degenerate into that.

2. Rising above the offence

There is another and very different way of dealing with wrongdoing without either hating or forgiving. It involves turning away from consideration of the wrongdoer and focusing instead on the state of mind of the victim. The victim is often filled with anger and resentment at the perpetrator, and this is part of the burden that she labours under as a result of the offence. One way in which she may come to be free of it is for her to rise above the offence, to leave it behind so that it no longer dominates her mind and shapes her experience of life. Victims may come to do this in a variety of ways, most obviously through indifference and forgetfulness. As time passes, the victim may come to care less about the offence and the offender; she may lose her hostility to him because she has simply become indifferent. Eventually she may well forget about it all. This attitude is different from one of forgiveness, since it involves no well-wishing towards the offender. But is it in any way preferable? Does it avoid any of the objections to forgiveness that we looked at in Chapter 2?

First off, indifference and forgetting do seem to meet at least some of Nietzsche's objections to forgiveness. They don't involve any pretence that harming or wronging the victim doesn't matter, or that the victim's needs and rights are unimportant, or that the offender's failure to respect her is of lesser importance than re-establishing good relations between victim and wrongdoer. Perhaps indifference and forgetfulness that result primarily from the passage of time are an unstable response to wrongdoing, since memory may always be triggered again. But a more radical and also more stable version of rising above the offence can be seen in Nietzsche's account of the admirably strong person, the "higher man", the one who can rise above resentment and anger because he's unconcerned about the opinions and actions of those who try to harm him. Such a person will never feel resentment, because he simply doesn't care about the opinions of others; they're of no importance to him, and hence his status in his own eyes (which is all that matters to him) isn't affected by the attitudes, however hostile, that others take. He may fight them and indeed crush them if he feels the need to, but he won't resent them; that would simply be beneath him – his pride would not permit it. An early version of this character can be found in Aristotle's depiction of the "great-souled" man, the one who knows his own greatness and is untroubled by the pinpricks of hostility from others. (And recent versions abound in the popular literature and film of the twentieth and twenty-first centuries. The lone man on a mission; the self-sufficient action hero who may crush the opposition but is untroubled by it; the solitary genius who cares nothing for social convention: these are all familiar figures of both popular and high art.)

What are we to make of this response to wrongdoing, this rising above the offence by means of a sublime indifference to the offender? Is it preferable to forgiveness, does it provide a satisfactory resolution of the aftermath of conflict? The idealizing of self-sufficiency and pride and indifference to others involved in this view very often amounts to the endorsement of arrogance and self-admiration, and a failure of empathy and solidarity. Outside the pages of fiction, it's hard to see these characteristics as virtues. In particular, self-sufficiency as an ideal is both impossible and undesirable. (Nietzsche recognizes this in his critique of forgiveness, but his higher man seems nonetheless to value and aim at self-sufficiency.) Human beings are sociable animals, and the conditions of our lives make it impossible for us to live alone without help from others. In any case our relationships with others offer some of the greatest goods, the most deeply satisfying experiences, that human life can contain. The development of a character that is indifferent to or denies all this doesn't look like a promising way for us to deal with wrongdoing.

Furthermore, for some offences this whole approach would be morally objectionable, and indeed well-nigh impossible to carry out. Who would even consider asking the mother of a murdered child to rise above the offence, to become indifferent to what was done? Whatever objections there might be to suggesting that a person in her position might forgive the perpetrator, at least forgiveness wouldn't involve her ceasing to care about the killing of her child. The idea of rising above the offence as a general policy for treating wrongdoers becomes grossly, disgustingly, inappropriate once the offences are serious enough. As a way of responding to wrongdoing, this approach can't give proper weight to the demands of justice; nor can it acknowledge that "moving on" from the offence can be morally inappropriate; nor does it even recognize the moral nature of what was done to the victim. Except for relatively minor offences, there seems little to recommend it.

3. Reconciliation as a political necessity

Where the wrongdoing, and the conflict it creates, has involved not only individuals but whole groups of people, as in a civil war, then the issue of handling the aftermath is peculiarly pressing. In these circumstances the victims can't choose to banish the offenders from their lives: they have to live seeing their attackers, and the murderers of their children, every day. Somehow they have to find a way to bear this, and indeed that whole society has to find a way to live with the terrible past. One way, the way of justified retributive punishment reached through due legal process, is sometimes simply impossible. There are different reasons why this may be so. Sometimes amnesty for the perpetrators, and a promise that they won't be severely punished, is part of a deal struck between the conflicting parties, a deal that brings the conflict to an end less bloodily than would otherwise be the case, thereby to some extent

protecting the victims and reducing the number of future ones –
but at the price of justice. Something like this happened in the overthrow of the apartheid system in South Africa, which involved a
transition to democracy that was almost entirely bloodless, partly
because the promised amnesty for those who ran that oppressive
system played a role in their decision not to continue to fight for
its survival.

A different reason why retributive justice may be impossible is
that in the aftermath of large-scale atrocities, the numbers of perpetrators involved in them may simply overwhelm the justice system;
the courts are unable to cope with the volume of traffic, and the
prisons remain filled, perhaps for years on end, with people accused
of the most hideous crimes. This was the case in Rwanda, where
ten years after the overthrow of the genocidaires there were still
tens of thousands of detainees in prison, and no likelihood of their
getting a fair trial, or indeed any trial at all; nor was there any likelihood of the victims seeing justice done for their terrible injuries
and bereavements. But Rwanda, like South Africa before it, and like
other states dealing with the aftermath of terrible internal conflict,
had somehow to find a way in which the perpetrators could be
reintegrated into society, in ways which the victims found at least
tolerable. The aim here was reconciliation, so that communal life
could be resumed: without justice, but also without the threat of
bloody retribution.

There were significant differences between the Rwandan
gacaca system of community courts, and the South African Truth
and Reconciliation Commission, and forgiveness played a rather
different role in each of them. In South Africa, the Truth and
Reconciliation Commission operated under the aegis of its chair,
the anti-apartheid activist and Nobel Peace Prize-winner Bishop
Desmond Tutu, whose encouragement of forgiveness was strong
and influential. In Rwanda, by contrast, many of the churches had
been seriously implicated in the killings, and hence Christian pres-

sure in favour of forgiveness did not have the same credibility there. Nonetheless, in both cases forgiveness by the victims was encouraged by the authorities, and many people (especially outsiders) saw forgiveness as an integral part of reconciliation.

It's understandable after devastating conflicts that state authorities should make the restoration of social order one of their principal aims, and that they should promote forgiveness as the route to the reconciliation needed for that order. But do reconciliation and forgiveness go hand in hand? If we manage to get reconciliation after such enmity, have we thereby delivered forgiveness, with all its implications of goodwill and moral virtue?

There are in fact serious difficulties in assuming that the two must necessarily go together. First, reconciliation needn't imply forgiveness. Recognizing that we may need to be reconciled with our enemies in order to prevent future conflict is not the same as saying we need to forgive them. Reconciliation doesn't require goodwill on the victims' part, but simply a willingness to get along with their erstwhile oppressors for the sake of peace. This is not a morally negligible thing to do in the aftermath of atrocity, and we shouldn't underestimate the burden it places on victims, most of whom will have to forgo justice for the brutal wrongs that have been done to them. Still, it isn't the same thing as forgiveness, and shouldn't be confused with it.

Second, forgiveness needn't always involve reconciliation. An abused woman may genuinely forgive her violent partner, but quite properly refuse to be fully reconciled with him because of the danger to which this might expose her. Even where there are no reasons of prudence to block reconciliation, it may still be intrinsically inappropriate in the wake of certain crimes, even where forgiveness has taken place. Consider the possibility of forgiving a Nazi who was no longer a threat to humanity: Goebbels, let's say, were he to have become fully contrite and repentant (which of course never happened). It would be one thing to forgive him in these circumstances, but it would be quite another to have him round to dinner. Reconciliation involves a readiness to share the daily round with the offender, to accept him as a partner in the ordinary activities of life, but this is something that may not make sense in the shadow of the torture chambers, the death camps, the killing fields. Some crimes are so terrible that they leave something like a stain on the soul, which even human forgiveness cannot wash away. Perhaps it might be possible to forgive Goebbels, or Pol Pot, the instigator of the Cambodian genocide, or Josef Stalin, who presided over the deaths of millions in the gulags: it might be possible to wish that their lives go better; it might even – hard though this is to see – be right to do so; but their activities in the service of unimaginable suffering and death may have put them beyond real human reconciliation. There are some journeys from which there is no full return.

Finally, enterprises aiming at political reconciliation may often fail to achieve either justice or forgiveness. In return for the truth, the South African Truth and Reconciliation Commission often asked victims to give up their resentment while waiving the demand for just punishment for the perpetrators. But this kind of request might in fact add to the wrongs done to the victims, putting them under moral pressure to "forgive and forget", even though they have been denied justice. Victims who participated in the proceedings of the Truth and Reconciliation Commission were not required to forgive those who had wronged them, but they were often encouraged to do so, and greatly praised if they did. Those who refused to forgive were treated as people who, very understandably, had not yet managed to overcome their harmful resentments, who were still trapped in the past, to their own detriment and to that of the wider community. This is a view of resentment and the refusal to forgive that sees it as basically pathological, as primarily a barrier to individual and social recovery from conflict, and as a condition that, although psychologically understandable and excusable, has no real moral justification. On this picture, there are only two alternatives:

forgiveness, which is morally admirable and offers us all hope for the future; and resentment, in which the victim remains absorbed in her own injuries and seeks revenge for them in ways that are damaging both to herself and to the wider community. But this is a gross oversimplification of the range of possible responses to wrongdoing. As we have seen, resentment can often be driven not by the victim's concern for her own wrongs, but by a wider resistance to the violation of moral principles and standards, a resistance that may be socially valuable and that certainly shouldn't be morally dismissed.

In circumstances where the provision of justice isn't possible, reconciliation in its absence may be necessary to enable people to coexist minimally: to share a state and live together without further bloodshed. But to tie reconciliation too closely to forgiveness, and to imply that victims who refuse to forgive are morally or psychologically or socially defective, may be to add to the wrongs those victims have already suffered; and indeed some victims who participated in reconciliation procedures found that the pressure to forgive generated further anger and resentment in them, rather than helping to reduce it.

So what can we now conclude about the possibility of finding a third way, neither forgiveness nor punishment, as a response to wrongdoing and to resolve its aftermath? As we have seen, looking for greater understanding of the offender is valuable in itself, and sometimes it may help us work out how to prevent future offences. Sometimes, too, it may show us that there was indeed an excuse for what the offender did, and in those cases we should mitigate or even withhold blame entirely. But understanding offences mustn't in general be used to excuse, or worse still condone, what was done, and so understanding the causes won't on its own show us how to resolve the bitter resentment and hatreds that come in their wake. Again, rising above the offence and becoming indifferent to the offender may sometimes be appropriate, but as a general policy it will in many cases be morally offensive: for some wrong-doings, we demean the victims and ourselves if we become indifferent to or forgetful of the moral gravity of what was done to them. Reconciliation may in some circumstances be a social necessity, but it isn't the same as forgiveness; nor does it require it. Inevitably it glosses over the demands of justice, and if forgiveness is seen as the route to reconciliation then the consequent pressure to forgive the perpetrators is liable to impose further harm on victims, whose wrongs are already great, and who will not find justice in the reconciliation procedure.

Each of the proposed attempts to avoid the choice between forgiveness and resentment presents serious moral problems of its own. It's time now to return to forgiveness, and to see if a closer consideration of its nature can help us to resolve the problems it seems to present.

4. The case for forgiveness I: what the psychologists say

Before we return to the more philosophical debate, we should pause to consider what we can learn about forgiveness from empirical research. In recent years, work by psychologists on the topic of forgiveness has become a growth industry (if you visit the American Psychological Association's website and type in the word "forgiveness", you'll find over 150 results straight off). The hope behind some of these projects is that we'll be able to find ways to encourage conflict resolution, especially in countries torn apart by racial or ethnic violence. Substantial backing for such research is provided by, among others, the United Nations; forgiveness is one of the topics it supports, alongside research primarily concerned with relieving the pain and distress suffered by victims. Some studies focus on forgiveness in close personal relationships, especially marriage, while others are directed towards forgiveness by and between groups. Yet others study self-forgiveness, and at least one project looks at the issue from the perspective of the perpetrator rather than the victim, and asks what motivates perpetrators to seek forgiveness.

While the emphasis varies from group to group, for nearly all the psychologists engaged in these projects, theoretical research is undertaken with a therapeutic aim. They want to understand how forgiveness works in order to make it easier for people to forgive, because they think that forgiveness is likely to help healing of both victims and remorseful perpetrators, and to resolve conflicts. They want to develop what psychologists call "forgiveness interventions": strategies that people can employ on their own, or with the aid of a therapist, or in a group, that will help them learn how to forgive. Some of what the psychologists find out about forgiveness is relevant to the ethical discussion we're engaged in here, about whether forgiveness is what we should be aiming. But some of it is not, sometimes because it makes unjustified assumptions about resentment and forgiveness, sometimes because what it talks about turns out, once we look at it closely, not to be forgiveness at all. And sometimes psychological research on forgiveness, while perfectly legitimate as research, just doesn't bear on our central question about whether it's always right to forgive. So first we need to ask: what is it we can learn from psychology about forgiveness, and, just as importantly, what is it we can *not* learn?

What we can and can't learn from psychology

- We *cannot* learn from psychology what things are good or bad, nor which actions are right or wrong. We can't, therefore, discover from psychology itself whether forgiveness is always a good thing, nor what moral reasons there are to do it.
- We *cannot* learn from psychology what forgiveness is, although we can learn more about what people *believe* it is.
- We *can* study the psychological effects of forgiving and not forgiving, particularly on the forgiver but also on the person who is forgiven.
- Finally, we *can* learn from psychology what hinders people from forgiving and what in contrast helps them. And so we can learn how to help people forgive, if that's our aim.

We'll look at each of these in turn.

1. Psychology and the moral standing of forgiveness

Why can't psychology tell us whether forgiveness is a good thing? The reason is that psychology is a science, and the job of science is to explain what actually happens, not to decide whether what happens is good or bad. Science tells us how the world *is*, but there's nothing in the scientific method that can help tell us how the world *ought* to be. So psychology studies how people do behave, not how they ought to behave. It looks at human behaviour to find out what makes people tick, but it can't, by itself, say anything about whether it's good or bad for them to tick that way. We shouldn't, of course, complain that science can't tell us what's valuable and what isn't, or how we ought to behave; that simply isn't its job. In order to do their work, however, psychologists and other social scientists often make various assumptions about what's good and what's bad. That's not a problem, so long as we remember that that's all they are: assumptions. And assumptions can be challenged.

So, for example, most psychological studies simply assume that reduction in anxiety, anger and fear is good, and that reconciliation between opposing groups is a worthwhile goal. And often this is right. But psychology can't by itself tell us whether these things are always desirable, always a good thing. And if they aren't always a good thing, we'll need to know when they are and when they aren't, and psychology can't tell us that either; that's an issue in ethics, not in psychology. In so far as psychologists who study forgiveness are also interested in therapy, whose goal is the relieving of mental suffering and distress, they may have an understandable tendency to think that it's *always* good to get rid of "negative" emotions, such as guilt, grief or anger. Very often it is, but, as the case against forgiveness powerfully argues, there are circumstances in which these emotions are warranted and appropriate. Furthermore, failure to feel them on some occasions is itself a *moral* failure. A father who has tormented and abused his innocent children *ought* to feel guilty

65

about what he's done, and it's a further moral failure in him if he doesn't. A rich person, who gives none of his wealth to people who are less fortunate than he is, but who feels occasional pangs of guilt about this, is *right* to do so, and it would be even better if he felt enough of them to actually do something about it. To suppose that getting rid of negative emotions is always a good thing is to make an unwarranted and highly implausible moral assumption.

Psychologists are very often interested in what are sometimes termed "coping strategies": ways in which a person can learn to live with obstacles, frustration, loss, or depression. Successful coping strategies may relieve inner mental turmoil, lethargy, or distress and increase motivation, and what psychologists like to call, rather grandly, "positive affect" (by which they mean feeling good). But not all coping strategies are morally equal. For example, popular magazines are full of interviews with rock stars or Hollywood glitterati who, having run through a string of marriage partners, or having engaged in drug abuse that has hurt people they love, announce that therapy has taught them how to get over what they have done, accept themselves and move on. The assumption behind all this is that the proper, healthy, response to behaving in irresponsible or cruel or thoughtless ways is to learn to accept yourself, as if being comfortable in your own skin is all that matters. But those who have suffered as a result of this behaviour have now disappeared from view, as if they were of no importance at all. The deep self-centredness of this version of the therapeutic approach is morally objectionable, no matter how comfortable it makes the person who is so ready to forgive himself. The unexamined assumption that accepting yourself is the most important thing blinds those who make that assumption to how morally objectionable this attitude is.

Similarly, various moral assumptions that are not argued for, and are sometimes clearly unjustified, can be found in some of the psychological literature on forgiveness. First, as we've suggested, many studies simply assume that any therapy that reduces negative emotions such as anger in the victims of wrongdoing, and makes them feel better about themselves, is an unqualifiedly good thing. Indeed, some go further and talk of "relinquishing anger as a psychological defence" as if anger were, by its very nature, not a morally fitting response to wrongdoing, but a mere coping strategy, and an ineffective one at that. But one of the central questions in the forgiveness debate is whether anger is sometimes a justified response – the *right* response – to wrongdoing, and studies that simply take it for granted that anger is never right and appropriate are assuming the very question at issue.

Second, these studies, because they occur in a therapeutic context, tend to assume that the *aim* of forgiveness is to reduce or get rid of psychological states that distress the victim, or make it hard for him to get on with his life. So there's a real danger of thinking of forgiveness interventions as part of the great self-help industry. Just as you may want to lose weight, or learn to be more self-confident, or learn how to say no – because these changes will make your life go better – so you may want to give up your anger and resentment so that you can get on with your life. And here the forgiveness counsellor, like the personal trainer or the assertiveness therapist, may be seen as offering you the means of change. Let go of the bad feelings and move on.

Now forgiveness often does have the effect of making the person feel better, and that – given the horrible things that may have happened to the victim – is generally a very desirable thing. But as we've already seen, coming to feel better needn't be the aim or purpose of forgiveness at all, although it may be a very valuable side effect. Advocating forgiveness as a form of self-help therapy leaves out a huge part of the moral dimension of forgiveness because it leaves the wrongdoer out of the equation. From the moral point of view, if forgiveness is admirable, it's admirable because it's a good response to the wrongdoer, despite what he's done to you. Forgiving is a form of moral activity – moral work, so to speak – that involves overcoming a natural, and justifiable, response of resentment and even hate, and replacing it with a morally admirable one of good-will, or even love. The danger is that, on the therapeutic model, the focus is solely on the welfare of the victim. The moral work of forgiveness is replaced with a piece of mental hygiene: a spring-cleaning of unwanted lumber from the mental attic.

A central issue in the debate about forgiveness is whether it is indeed a morally admirable response to injury, or whether a focus on justice and punishment is morally preferable. But if we think of forgiveness merely as a form of self-help, then how can we see it as a genuinely moral achievement at all? The great moral prophets of forgiveness – people of the stature of Buddha, Jesus, Gandhi, or Martin Luther King – offer us an exalted and exalting picture of love for our enemies and persecutors as a resoundingly moral response to what they have done to us. What makes their lives inspiring moral examples is that they were lived for others; they were precisely not focused on self, still less on learning how to feel better about themselves.

Some of the psychologists who advocate "forgiveness interventions" are aware of this criticism and attempt to rebut it. Thus one group writes that there is a:

> large difference between traditional therapies and forgiveness therapy: No therapy before forgiveness therapy has deliberately taken the spot-light off the client and pointed it straight at the offender. The client in forgiveness therapy must step outside of a primary self-focus toward a moral focus on the offender. As paradoxical as this seems for therapy, it works.
> (Freedman *et al.* 2005: 401)

But the final emphasis here on what *works* suggests that the therapeutic aim, with its focus on the needs of the forgiver, is still ultimately in the driving seat. Other psychologists are quite explicit about their exclusively therapeutic focus. The second aim of the Stanford Forgiveness Project reads: "Make a commitment to yourself to do what you have to do to feel better. Forgiveness is for you *and not for anyone else*" (American Psychological Association 2008: 15, emphasis added).

Robert Enright, who heads up one of the largest groups working in this area, the Forgiveness Institute, strenuously denies that forgiveness is merely an act motivated by self-interest. The Forgiveness Institute website shows commendable awareness of the moral dimensions of forgiveness, talking of it as a generous gift to the wrongdoer, one that seeks to overcome wrongdoing with good. However, the model to which the researchers appeal in the "Enright Forgiveness Inventory", which is designed by the Institute as the working basis for therapeutic intervention, sends a very different message. Here the emphasis seems almost exclusively on the benefits to the forgiver, and not on the appropriateness of the response. "What can it do for you?" is the question that is addressed. Forgetting, rather than forgiving, is regarded as undesirable because it won't stop the victim being abused again. There is a strong correlation, we're told, between failing to forgive and depression, while those who forgive experience an increase in "positive well-being". It's bad for victims to feel anger, shame, or guilt, because "these reactions can deplete their energy".

Here a therapeutic and self-interested understanding of forgiveness still seems to be dominant, in spite of the official line taken by the Institute. This kind of psychological research can't help us establish whether forgiveness is always right, because it assumes that the point of forgiveness is therapeutic, and it assumes that therapy is always justified. But these are among the central issues of the debate about forgiveness. We can't resolve the questions of whether the best reason for forgiveness is a therapeutic one, and whether forgiveness is always right, simply by *assuming* that the answer to them is yes.

2. What is forgiveness?

Why can't psychology tell us what forgiveness is? The reason is that forgiveness, a complex phenomenon that isn't easy to define or analyse, is a rich part of our moral lives, and we have a working grip on what it is quite independently of any psychological research. If the account of forgiveness with which researchers are working doesn't capture the main elements of our non-specialist concept, then it's not clear that they're really researching on the same subject. And if they aren't, then their findings won't help to advance our understanding of forgiveness. So it really matters that the psychological researcher gets her definitions right, and uses them consistently in her research. The usefulness of her work on forgiveness, as on any topic, will be affected by the clarity and accuracy of the operational definition she gives of the target of her enquiry. If her account of the phenomenon to be studied is confused, then her results will also be confused. And if she is actually studying something slightly different from what she takes herself to be studying, then her results, although they may be illuminating, won't illuminate their chosen target. What's needed for a good analysis of forgiveness is careful, morally sensitive reflection on the phenomenon. The specialist experimental skills of the psychologist don't in themselves put her in a position to give a better account of forgiveness than anyone else. And in practice, most psychologists, in constructing their definitions, refer to the philosophical literature.

The Forgiveness Institute give the most nuanced theoretical account of forgiveness (even though, as we have seen, this isn't always mirrored in their practice). They define forgiveness as a response to an injustice in which the forgiver retains an attitude of goodwill to the offender, and foregoes resentment and revenge, even though the wrongdoer's actions deserve this response. Forgiveness is not a duty but goes beyond duty, as a free gift to the offender. It is to be distinguished from forgetting, denying, condoning, and excusing.

It is incompatible with "rubbing in" your own moral superiority. It is also different from reconciliation: forgiveness is one person's moral response to another's injustice, whereas reconciliation, they say, requires both parties to come together in mutual respect (see www.forgiveness-institute.org/html/about_forgiveness.htm).

Their account presupposes, however, that all forgiveness is unconditional: that it doesn't depend on the wrongdoer's prior repentance. Not only is forgiveness a free gift but, they say, it "is not a quid pro quo deal – it doesn't demand compensation first". But this is a mistake. Conditional forgiveness is still forgiveness. Being willing to forgive only if the wrongdoer apologizes, repents and makes amends is still a willingness to *forgive*. Certainly there's an important moral question about whether we *should* forgive unconditionally, or whether it's morally better to reserve forgiveness only for those who have repented of their wrongdoings. But that moral issue is quite different from the question of whether conditional forgiveness is nonetheless forgiveness. In fact it clearly is, and indeed many people think it's morally preferable to unconditional forgiveness.

Of course, it's perfectly proper for researchers to restrict their research project to unconditional forgiveness if they want to, but they shouldn't make that restriction a matter of definition; our account of the nature of forgiveness shouldn't depend on what topics researchers prefer to work on. It turns out, however, that the identification of forgiveness with unconditional forgiveness isn't an accidental oversight, but stems from the researchers' focus on therapeutic concerns. Enright points out that to make forgiveness conditional is to place great power in the hands of the offender, who, by refusing to accommodate the demands of the victim for repentance, can prevent the victim from obtaining the release she hopes forgiveness will give her. So Enright's objection to conditional forgiveness is simply a therapeutic one – it may be bad for the forgiver – rather than a moral one. Holding out for apology or reparation might damage the victim. Once again we see that the therapeutic approach presupposes that the main, if not the only, question in deciding whether or not to forgive is: what will it do for me? But this focus on what forgiveness can do for you misses the moral context of the decision to forgive. As Anthony Bash nicely puts it: "Forgiveness is a moral issue with psychological implications; it is not a psychological issue with moral undertones" (Bash 2007: 46).

Another weakness of the Enright Forgiveness Inventory is that it holds that *all* negative attitudes must be relinquished in forgiveness, including anger, indignation and sadness. Thus in their questionnaire the presence of negative feelings such as anger, dislike or disgust indicate lack of forgiveness. And forms of behaviour such as ignoring, neglecting, not attending to, not speaking to or staying away from the offender are also taken to indicate the absence of forgiveness, as are beliefs and attitudes such as disapproving of the wrongdoer, condemning him and thinking him bad, evil, corrupt, wretched or immoral. But treating these responses as showing that the responder hasn't forgiven undercuts the good points that the Forgiveness Institute make in their definition of forgiveness. There they rightly insist that forgiving is not condoning, but rather involves recognizing that a wrong has been done. But to recognize that someone has done a serious wrong is to disapprove of and to condemn that person, at least for that action. And the victim may be correct in thinking that the wrongdoer is bad, or corrupt, or even evil – some wrongdoers really are like this – but these thoughts don't by themselves rule out forgiveness, since it's possible (although not easy) to forgive someone whom you recognize to be a bad person.

The scoring of the inventory, by contrast with the Forgiveness Institute's official views on forgiveness, not only conflates forgiving and condoning, but seems to require that, in some cases at least, the victim should come to have rose-coloured beliefs about the moral status of the offender that will often be simply false. But this is a view that certainly won't help us to think of forgiveness as being morally admirable: we don't normally think it's admirable to believe in falsehoods, however positive and optimistic they are. Another mismatch between the theory and the practice occurs where the Forgiveness Institute account rightly insists that forgiveness isn't the same as, and doesn't require, reconciliation. Yet, according to the inventory, one who ignores, does not speak to or stays away from the offender shows that he has not fully forgiven. But this amounts to saying that reconciliation is needed for forgiveness after all. The inventory fails, by its own lights, to measure accurately the thing it claims to be investigating.

Other research projects do a less good job in defining forgiveness. It's often confused with condoning or excusing. This confusion can be encouraged by an emphasis on what psychologists call "reframing". In reframing, the person who has been wronged tries to understand the wrongdoer's act from the wrongdoer's point of view. The thought here is that once the wrongdoer's act becomes explicable it will be more easily forgivable. Maybe so, if the victim has misjudged the wrongdoer. But certainly not always. Indeed, the more the victim understands, the worse she may (correctly) come to think the wrongdoer is, and hence the less she may wish to forgive. Richard McCann, the son of one of the serial killer Peter Sutcliffe's victims, concluded that Sutcliffe "was simply evil and no longer deserving of his time and energy". Think also of Jean Girumuhatse, the Rwandan genocidaire who revelled in his killings. Does understanding his sense of increased power in the kingdom of death that Rwanda became make him seem more forgivable?

Some psychologists even go so far as to claim that if an action can be understood, it must make sense from the agent's perspective, and so it must be acceptable. Thus Ellen Langer says that the perpetrator's behaviour "makes sense from the actor's [that is, the wrongdoer's] perspective, or else it would not have occurred. I am right, and so are you" (quoted in Bash 2007: 43; see also www.ellen-langer.com/blog/139/blaming-the-victim). But this is a dreadful argument, and it leads to an appalling conclusion. Langer is moving from the thought that the perpetrator must have had a goal or aim that made sense of his action to the thought that his action must be morally acceptable. But not all comprehensible actions or goals are morally acceptable. My action can make sense, and still be wrong. Forgiveness doesn't require the forgiver to think that "I am right, and so are you"; that would be to equate forgiving with excusing or condoning. This is psychobabble of the kind that brought us "I'm OK; you're OK", an attitude beautifully satirized in *The Mikado* by W. S. Gilbert: "And I am right / And you are right / And all is right as right can be!"

But if we're all of us right, then there's nothing to forgive, and nothing even to complain about. This is a total travesty of the real nature of wrongdoing, and the seriousness, and sometimes the enormity, of what has happened to the victim. It's the kind of view that does indeed give forgiveness a bad name.

Failing to be clear about the definition of the thing one is studying can make us vulnerable to another mistake, namely, carrying out research that purports to discover something we already knew just by thinking about the subject matter of the study. Suppose a researcher were to apply for a grant to discover if all depressed people had a less positive outlook on life than those who aren't depressed. The grant-awarding authority would (we hope) laugh this proposal out of court, pointing out that we already know this if we understand what depression is, and so we don't need to do a study to find it out. Defining forgiveness, as we have seen, isn't easy, but everyone agrees that it requires the cessation of hostile feelings towards the wrongdoer. And a study has been carried out (American Psychological Association 2008: 20–22), which showed, among other things, that "anger-related emotions (hostility and resentment, rather than other negative emotions, such as fear and disgust) hinder forgiveness". Clearly the researchers in this study had forgotten the definition of their topic. They didn't need to waste time and money to discover *that*!

Psychology can also find out what ordinary people take forgiveness to be. While that doesn't determine how best to define it – since people can be muddled and mistaken in this as in any area – it's important to discover whether the account that we're working with isn't too far away from the popular picture, to ensure that we're all still talking about the same phenomenon. The results here seem to be rather mixed. The most common response to the question "What is forgiveness?" was that it involved "letting go of negative feelings and grudges". On the other hand, some research in attitudes has been taken to suggest that a majority thought that forgiveness and retributive justice were incompatible. But a closer examination of the data doesn't really support this interpretation. Sixty per cent of respondents considered the statement, "If you really forgive someone, you would want that person to be released from the consequences of their actions," to be accurate (Fincham 2009: 367). The problem with this finding, however, is that the question is very loosely and ambiguously phrased, and hence we can't be certain of what exactly the answers show. What consequences did people who agreed with this statement have in mind? Perhaps some were thinking not of just punishment, but of other things one might do to those against whom one has a grudge, such as shunning them, or holding the offence against them, or expelling them from previously shared groups or communities. That thought highlights a problem that besets all research in this area, namely, the difficulty of devising questionnaires that really measure what it is we want to measure.

Why is it so difficult? There are a number of reasons: first, it's very hard to frame questions or statements that are sufficiently clear and unambiguous so that almost all respondents will understand them in the way the researchers intended. We might do this by clarifying, expanding and explaining the statements on the questionnaire, but that introduces its own problems: the questionnaire can become too confusing, or too hard to understand, or simply too long to be practicable.

Second, if we're examining some psychological state, or character trait, we need to ask questions about patterns of behaviour, feelings and attitudes that we take to be correlated with the psychological feature we are looking at. But in the case of forgiveness, this is difficult. We need not only to have the right account of forgiveness, but also to ensure that our questions match our account: that the questions don't focus on attitudes, beliefs, feelings or traits that aren't really relevant to the account. As we've seen with the Enright Forgiveness Inventory, this isn't always an easy thing to do.

Third, character traits such as forgiveness can be displayed in different ways by different people. Take generosity. In one person, this might take the form of responding to individual requests for help whenever someone makes them. In a second, it might take the form of contributing a substantial portion of his salary to reputable charities, but then refusing all individual requests for assistance. In a third person, there might be some combination of these two. All these patterns of behaviour (and many more) could count as exemplifications of generosity, so it's not going to be easy to compare one person's generosity with another's; but unless we can do that, we won't be able to do research on it.

Fourth, desirable character traits, the sort that we think of as virtues, will enable the agent to have a flexible response to the events she encounters. That's because the virtuous agent needs to be able to respond appropriately to a very wide variety of situations. In the case of love, for example, what will count as the loving response will vary enormously, depending on exactly what the situation is that the loving person faces. Love may require inflexibility here but flexibility there; it might involve being sympathetic to one person but strict with another, and so on and so forth. If forgiveness is a virtue, then just what it requires us to do will vary from case to case. Sometimes the forgiving person will pass over something in silence; sometimes he will protest. Sometimes he will seek reconciliation, and sometimes not. The problem for the psychologist is to devise a measurement tool that's sufficiently sensitive to the varying responses that the forgiving person will make in differing circumstances. But if the variations are too complex, or too subtle, it may prove impossible to capture them in any manageable measurement tool.

3. The psychological effects of forgiving

A more promising area in which psychological research can be of help to us is in exploring the connection between forgiveness and well-being. Since some of the claims in the forgiveness debate focus directly on the supposed therapeutic powers of forgiveness, it certainly would be helpful to know just how great these powers are. To study this, researchers will try to find correlations between having a tendency to be forgiving and reporting high levels of personal satisfaction. However this kind of research, like the ones we've already looked at, suffers from problems with devising measurement tools. The difficulty here is that a tendency to forgive may be associated with other personality traits, and what we may be measuring may not be a connection between being *forgiving* and judging that your life is going well, but between some other trait associated with forgiving and satisfaction with your life. So yet further studies have to be done to ensure that it is the tendency to forgive that is causally connected to the satisfaction, and not some other trait. (This last point is well illustrated in the final study we look at.)

We've seen that the focus in forgiveness interventions is largely on the welfare of victims. The assumption is that their lives are improved by forgiveness, and so the focus of research is on how to learn to forgive. But interestingly one study (American Psychological Association 2008: 17–19) suggested, in connection with the attack on the World Trade Center, that those who suffered the most psychological distress and turmoil were those who were ambivalent about forgiveness. The study divided respondents into three categories: those who had already forgiven, or were trying to do so; those who were clear that forgiveness was inappropriate; and those who had not made up their mind either way. Those who forgave did best in terms of the goals laid down in the study, which included avoiding involuntary thinking about the event, being able to control one's emotional reactions and finding meaning in the event. But those in the anti-forgiveness camp experienced less distress than those who were ambivalent. Here we can see that in some circumstances the refusal to forgive may help people more than some of the available alternatives.

However at least one psychologist, James McNulty, has gone further, and expressed direct scepticism about the claims of positive psychology in general, and the healing powers of forgiveness in particular. The kinds of claims about which he's so dubious are well expressed in this example from one of the many books on positive psychology, which explains the theory behind this movement as follows:

> The field of positive psychology at the subjective level is about valued subjective experiences: well-being, contentment, and satisfaction (in the past); hope and optimism (for the future) and flow and happiness (in the present). At the individual level, it is about positive individual traits: the capacity for love and vocation, courage, interpersonal skill, aesthetic sensibility, perseverance, forgiveness, originality, future mindedness, spirituality, high talent, and wisdom.
>
> (Seligman & Csikszentmihalyi 2000: 5)

McNulty has conducted a series of studies that challenge the claim that there are certain character traits and skills that always result in more happiness and better mental health. A corollary of this claim is that we should be able to make unhappy people happier by teaching them these skills, or by encouraging them to change their approach to, or outlook on, life. McNulty and others looked at a range of "positive" traits to see how they correlated with how people felt about themselves, their level of self-respect, and how others treated them. What they report is that whether people who have a "positive" outlook are happier, manage their lives better, or have good levels of self-respect, is highly context-dependent. So, for example, people who are skilled at some task perform even better if they have positive expectations about their performance, and experience increased levels of satisfaction, compared with people who lack confidence. But people who have poor skills and high expectations about their performance experience increased dissatisfaction, compared with people who have lower expectations. These results are not very surprising. If people are good at what they do, then believing they can go out there and do it will typically enable them to do their best, and so gain satisfaction. But wholly unrealistic beliefs about one's own skills are just going to lead to pratfalls and humiliation. It's true that the boosting of people's "self-esteem" has been treated as unquestionably desirable in popular psychologizing for some time now. But recent research in areas other than forgiveness is increasingly suggesting that high self-esteem and positive self-expectation don't necessarily correlate with high levels of satisfaction, and this shouldn't come as a surprise to anyone whose own good opinion of themselves has ever been mugged by a recalcitrant reality.

McNulty has conducted several studies on forgiveness with couples in the first four years of marriage. In the first study, people were rated for their degree of forgivingness, and couples were also asked to report on the frequency of negative behaviour. The study found that:

among spouses married to partners who infrequently engaged in negative behaviour, increased forgiveness appeared to be beneficial over time, whereas less forgiveness appeared to be harmful over time. In contrast ... among spouses married to partners who frequently engaged in negative behaviour, increased forgiveness appeared to be harmful over time, whereas decreased forgiveness appeared to be beneficial over time. (McNulty 2008: 173–4)

Two further studies showed similar results. In relationships in which people rated their partners as being agreeable, forgiveness led to a decrease in negative behaviour, whereas lack of forgiveness increased it. But in relationships where people rated their partners as less agreeable, that tendency was reversed. Those who were more forgiving found their partners behaved badly towards them more often. Finally, those who were more forgiving and in good relationships reported increased self-respect whereas those in less good relationships reported decreased self-respect. Conversely, the unforgiving who were in good relationships reported a decline in their self-respect, while the unforgiving in less good relationships reported an increase in their self-respect.

What conclusions should we draw from this? We might think, as McNulty seems inclined to do, that only in certain circumstances are "positive" traits such as forgivingness good for those who possess them. We have stressed, of course, that in any case the primary reason to forgive is not to make one's life go better. But it would be unfortunate if being forgiving actually made your life go worse. Happily we can resist this conclusion, in at least two ways. First, these studies leave out the thought that you might be a better person for having a forgiving nature, and so it would be desirable to be forgiving, even though it cost you something. (Here forgiveness is similar to another virtue, courage: this virtue may well cost you a lot, but you're still a better person with it, and it's still valuable.)

Psychological studies can't really address this possibility, since they primarily study measurable features, and neither they nor anybody else knows how to measure a normative state, such as being a better person.

Second, we have to remember that people can forgive for bad, trivial and facile reasons, as well as for noble and selfless ones. McNulty's study doesn't, as far as we can see, distinguish between the reasons people have for forgiving; it merely measures how much people are likely to forgive in various circumstances. But people sometimes forgive for bad reasons as well as good ones; it would be unsurprising, for example, if people who forgive because they are timid, supine or feebly subservient fared badly in relationships that were already struggling. The title of one of the studies is very revealing: "The Doormat Effect: When Forgiving Erodes Self-respect and Self-concept Clarity". Of course, if people forgive out of shallow and subservient motives, then their lives will probably not go well. But, as we'll go on to investigate more fully in later chapters, forgiveness is compatible with protest, indignation, standing up for yourself and "pushing back". There are forms of forgiveness that come from strength: the strength to do the moral work that forgiveness involves.

Gandhi wrote that "the weak can never forgive the strong; forgiveness is the attribute of the strong." If Gandhi is talking about moral strength, then we have to dissent from his claim. People can forgive out of moral weakness, but their forgiveness is likely to be unsatisfactory and unsatisfying. Shallow, facile forgiveness is a poor thing, although it may still be better than hatred and resentment, where that's allied to the gratifications of revenge rather than to justice. And although forgiving for the right reasons can't guarantee that our lives will go well, at least forgivers don't have to be regarded, or regard themselves, as doormats. Forgiving for the right reasons will involve moral strength, and that's the kind of forgiveness that will be admirable.

4. Psychological research on aids and barriers to forgiveness

Finally, psychology can certainly help us to find out which beliefs and attitudes assist forgiveness, and which ones hinder it. Forgiveness is hard. There are useful techniques that can help you overcome resentment, just as there are things you can do or think about that will make it harder. Psychological research can be of the first importance in discovering what these might be. So what we may hope to learn from "forgiveness interventions" is how best to help those who wish to forgive for the right reasons to achieve their aim. But this has very little direct bearing on the question we began with, the question of whether forgiveness is actually what we should be aiming at in the first place.

The debate about forgiveness with which we're concerned in this book centres on the question of whether forgiveness is always the right thing to do. What we can learn from the psychologists about this question turns out to be fairly limited: we can learn something about what people's views on forgiveness actually are; we can learn something about the extent to which its effects are indeed therapeutic; and we can learn rather more about what makes it easier or harder to forgive. But in all these cases the research will be hampered by the fact that forgiveness is so complex and multifaceted a phenomenon that capturing it for quantitative study is very difficult, and in any case researchers will need to resort to the ethical discussions of the subject in order to provide an adequate account of just what it is that's being measured. So we'll now return to these more philosophical approaches, to see if forgiveness can in the end be defended against the powerful critique of it which we looked at in earlier chapters.

5. The case for forgiveness II: meeting the objections

My personal task is to justify a psychic condition [resentment] which has been condemned by moralists and psychologists alike. The former regard it as a taint, the latter as a kind of sickness …

[But] when I stand by my resentments … I still know that I am the captive of the *moral truth* of the conflict. … The Flemish SS-man Wajs, who – inspired by his German masters – beat me on the head with a shovel handle whenever I didn't work fast enough, felt the tool to be an extension of his hand and the blows to be emanations of his psychophysical dynamics. Only I possessed, and still possess, the moral truth of the blows that even today still roar in my skull … my resentments are there in order that the crime become a moral reality for the criminal, in order that he be swept into the truth of his atrocity … (Améry 1980: 64, 69–70)

Anger drained away, in its place came a welling of compassion for both Nagase and for me, coupled with a deep sense of sadness and regret. … Forgiveness became more than an abstract idea: it was now a real possibility. … I began to appreciate how damaged he must have been by what he had done. … Nor was his concern to make reparation an occasional thing; it was truly almost a way of life. …

He looked up at me; he was trembling, in tears, saying over and over "I am very, very sorry". (Lomax 1995: 255, 263)

Both Jean Améry and Eric Lomax suffered hideous tortures at the hand of their captors. However Lomax's torturer eventually became filled with remorse for what he had done, and spent the remainder of his life trying to atone for it. These are the circumstances in which Lomax found it possible to forgive. Améry faced a world in which most of those who had been complicit in the Nazi horrors showed no such remorse, and he came to feel that only the preservation of resentment could do justice to, and maintain knowledge of, the moral truth of what had happened. His case, and that of many others, against forgiveness is a *moral* case: forgiveness is charged with being morally inadequate to the reality of wrongdoing, rather than just with being unattractive, or difficult to carry out, or in some other way psychologically unsatisfactory. If we're to find out whether this case can be answered then we'll have to think in more detail about just what forgiveness actually is, just which position it occupies in the complex network of our attitudes to others, just what it requires and what it rules out. Some conceptions of forgiveness are clearly glib and facile, and hence morally negligible (or worse). Is there a way of thinking about forgiveness that escapes the serious criticisms levelled at it, which can recognize the value of sustained resentment, and which can take into itself what we've learned from the case against forgiveness? Is there a conception of forgiveness that isn't cheap and easy, that doesn't short-change the weight and importance of the offence and of the victim herself? To answer these questions, we'll need to think again, and in rather more detail, about what is, and also what isn't, actually involved in the business of forgiving an offender.

What forgiveness is not

Very often, when we want to see the outline of a concept and what kind of thing it covers, we can do so by considering what sort of thing is close to it but nonetheless is distinct, and therefore falls outside the concept. If we want to understand what a whale is, we need to see how it differs from a fish; if we want to understand what counts as a liberal democracy, we need to see that it's not the same as pure majority rule. So to get a clearer conception of forgiveness, we need to look at its close neighbours, at things that bear some resemblance to it, but nonetheless are not identical. Some of the attitudes that don't amount to forgiveness (although as we've already seen they're sometimes confused with it) include condoning the offence, excusing it, ignoring it, forgetting it or "wiping the slate clean". We'll now need to look a little more closely at each of these to see how they differ from forgiveness, and thereby get a clearer idea of what forgiveness itself is like.

When we condone an action, we say in effect that it wasn't really such a bad thing to do. Here's an example of condoning:

> Did members of parliament take every penny they could get in expenses? Well, that wasn't really so bad, was it? No government ever wants to raise MPs' pay, because it's always unpopular with the electorate. So they had a very generous expenses scheme to make up their income. It wasn't such a terrible thing – the whole expenses scandal cost less than a decent pay rise for them would have done.

Condoning an action amounts to saying (correctly or incorrectly) that the action wasn't really wrong. But not only is this different from forgiveness, but it actually rules out forgiveness. If there's been no wrongdoing, then there's nothing to forgive. We certainly shouldn't go around forgiving people who haven't done anything wrong; it's intensely annoying for them, because of the false assumption that they're wrongdoers.

Condoning an action is not the same as excusing it. The two have one very important thing in common: both are ways of saying that the offender isn't to blame for what he did. But in other respects they're very different. Where condoning an action says that the action wasn't actually wrong, excusing the action amounts to saying that yes, it really was wrong, but the person who committed it wasn't to blame, because of his special circumstances. Sometimes the excuse is a good one that does really remove blame; there are often perfectly genuine excuses for people who do wrong (which includes most of us at some time or another), since life is often a difficult and complicated business. But bad excuses are common, and this shouldn't surprise us, since the principal purpose of any excuse is to deflect disapproval and punishment, and these are aims that blameworthy wrongdoers are likely to have, just as much as blameless ones.

Often the situation with respect to blame is quite complicated, with partial excuses alongside some measure of responsibility and blame. An example of excuse-making that captures this complexity beautifully, displaying an ironic understanding of how excuses can be manipulated and abused, can be found in Stephen Sondheim's lyrics for "Gee, Officer Krupke", from *West Side Story*. Here the gang members explain to the police why they're not to blame for their bad behaviour: it's all the fault of their drugged-up mothers and alcoholic fathers, the absence of love in their lives, the absence of psychotherapy, the absence of work. They claim that it's society's fault they have a "social disease", and the onlooker can to some extent accept this; but underneath these excuses it's also obvious that the gang members are mocking both the world outside the gangs and to some extent themselves. We both do and don't accept their excuses, just as the gang members both are and aren't sincere when they make them.

We shouldn't forget, however, that some excuses are very powerful indeed, and do serve to lift much or all of the blame for terrible actions from the shoulders of those who committed them. Here's one example of this kind of excuse, in a discussion of child soldiers:

Child soldiers are quite common in some areas of the world, particularly Africa, Asia and South America. The conditions that lead to their deployment are often, indeed usually, quite horrific. ... A group of armed men enters a village and gathers the inhabitants together in an open public space. A child of perhaps 10 years of age is selected and ordered to take a gun and kill his friend, or perhaps one of his parents. The first such child may hesitate or refuse, and is instantly shot dead. Another is then brought forward and given the same order. Those subsequently chosen are less likely to refuse. After a sufficient number of children have been put through this ordeal in full view of the entire village, they are taken away at gunpoint to a camp where they are to be turned into soldiers. Actually though, the process has already begun. It began with the coerced killings in the village, which have various effects: making the killer feel irredeemably corrupted, making him an outcast from his community, binding him to his abductors, and so on. ... At the camp, they are further brutalized, indoctrinated and trained, perhaps for several years. Finally they are given light automatic weapons and administered drugs that further anesthetize their consciences and subdue their fears, and are sent to fight for an unjust cause. ...

Children who have been subjected to these horrible abuses have unusually strong excuses.   (McMahan 2009: 199–200)

There's no question here of condoning what the child soldiers have done and will do: it's unequivocally horrible and wrong. But if ever anyone had an excuse that made it impossible to hold them fully responsible for what they do, and hence to fully blame them, it's these tragic children, who are as much casualties of war as those whom they attack.

The main thing to note about excusing is that it reduces, sometimes to nothing, the scope for forgiveness. If there's a full excuse for what the wrongdoer did, then he's not to blame for it. And if he isn't to blame, then there's nothing to forgive. Feelings of resentment or hatred that we may have towards the fully excused wrongdoer are in fact misplaced: the horrors that were enacted were truly not his fault. Because a full excuse has this dramatic consequence for our attitudes towards the wrongdoer, it takes quite a lot for such an excuse to be genuinely present. Often excuses are partial rather than full, and in those cases they lift some, although not all, of the blame from the offender's shoulders, so that something, although not the full weight of the offence, still remains to be forgiven. Ordinary private cases of wrongdoing are often like that: the sister who constantly snipes at you, who criticizes you to your parents and who never gives you the credit for doing anything well, may be a very insecure person who has to run others down in order to feel better about herself, and one of the causes of her insecurity may be that you were indeed the unfairly favoured child – your parents really did prefer you to her, and she's never been able to get over this. These are circumstances that may furnish a partial (although only a partial) excuse for her mean and begrudging behaviour to you. In more terrible kinds of wrongdoing, partial excuses may also be present, although of course the greater the wrongdoing the harder it is to excuse it, especially if the supposedly excusing conditions can be found in many people who don't in fact go on to commit great wrongdoings. Poverty and frustrated ambitions are not much of an excuse for mass murder if most poor people would never consider becoming murderers at all. However, cases of horrific action where there is a full excuse for the perpetrator, although rare, do exist, as we have seen with child soldiers; in such cases a wrongdoer is tragically hard to distinguish from a victim.

Forgiveness, unlike condoning or excusing, doesn't involve saying that the offence wasn't really so bad, or that the offender wasn't actually to blame for what he did. On the contrary, the forgiver has a clear-eyed view of what was wrong with the offender's action, and also of how responsible he was for committing the offence, and still manages to overcome hostility to him, and to wish him well. Sometimes it's difficult to see how people can actually do this, especially where the wrongdoing was really grave. Forgiveness is seriously hard.

For similar reasons, forgiveness won't involve either ignoring, or forgetting, what was done to the victim. When you forgive someone, you forgive them for something wrongful that they've done. This entails that you're aware of it, that you haven't either ignored it or forgotten about it. Of course, after forgiveness has taken place, and if the offence wasn't great, you may come to forget all about it (this can sometimes happen even if you don't forgive). But for a major offence – say, where someone has seriously harmed your child – it would be quite wrong to expect the victim to forget what had happened. Nonetheless, people in these circumstances do sometimes forgive the perpetrator, even though they may never forget what was done.

We've already considered (in Chapter 2) the view of forgiveness as "wiping the slate clean", and we've seen how unsatisfactory an account of forgiveness that is. Sometimes it may be appropriate after forgiveness to restore the situation to the way things were before the offence occurred, but often it won't be. If you keep borrowing my car, and keep bumping it into passing trees and lamp-posts, then I may (with a certain amount of effort) forgive you for this. But I needn't necessarily go on lending you my car: not because I'm full of hostility towards you – if I've forgiven you, that's just what I've overcome – but because I don't want my car to go on being damaged. Forgiving you doesn't mean ignoring the evidence about your terrible driving, or, in another kind of case, the evidence of your uncontrollable temper and readiness to resort to violence. Forgiveness doesn't require that victims continue to put themselves at risk, or that they ignore the evidence from the past when deciding how to act in the future.

But there is perhaps one aspect of forgiveness that does seem to involve something like wiping the slate clean. If I have forgiven, then I shouldn't keep bringing the offence up, and I won't be able to go on holding it against the offender. (If I find, as may often be the case, that I actually want to go on holding it against him, then I haven't really forgiven him at all. Many of us have depressingly personal experience of wanting to maintain a grudge, even against our better judgement.)

Since in forgiveness we need to know the nature of the offence (otherwise it's not clear what exactly is being forgiven), it won't involve any failure to take the offence seriously enough, or for that matter to take the victim seriously enough. The difficult and remarkable task of forgiveness is to see precisely how much the victim was wronged, how profound was the failure to respect her as she (like all persons) should be respected, and still to overcome hostility to the perpetrator.

So that's what forgiveness is not: it's not condoning or excusing or ignoring or forgetting or wiping out the past. In the light of that we can look again at the central features of forgiveness, and see what their implications are.

What forgiveness implies

Since forgiveness rules out condoning or excusing or ignoring the offence, it must involve a clear-sighted awareness of the nature of the wrongdoing and the offender's responsibility for it. In the light of that awareness, and in the presence of natural responses to wrongdoing, such as indignation, resentment and hatred, the forgiver overcomes all the responses that involve ill will, and adopts an attitude of at least minimal goodwill towards the person who has wronged her.

What follows from this two-part conception of forgiveness? What does it commit us to, and can it help us to address the powerful criticisms we met when we looked at the case against forgiveness in Chapter 2? There are at least three things that seem to follow straight away from this conception: first, indignation isn't ruled out, so the victim who forgives can still rightly feel indignant about the crime. Indignation isn't the same as hatred: the former is a kind of outrage about the violation of morality that the offence involved; hatred, by contrast, is a feeling of ferocious hostility to the perpetrator herself. Indignation normally involves the desire to protest against and to make good the breach in the moral law, and to take steps to prevent further breaches; but outrage at the violation of moral norms needn't involve ill will towards the wrongdoer. Perhaps that's most evident in parental relations: a father can quite consistently and comprehensibly say that he's appalled by what his son did, but he still loves him and wishes him well, and hopes he'll become a better person eventually. And this kind of attitude isn't confined to parents and children: one can feel about a friend that what she did was outrageous, and it should be protested in the strongest terms, but nonetheless you wish her well and hope for her future improvement. It's only hostile, ill-wishing attitudes to the wrongdoer that need to be given up in forgiveness, so we can see that indignation can be maintained by the forgiver, although hatred can't. What we have here is something rather like a secular analogue of the Christian injunction to hate the sin but love the sinner; we can be outraged by the wrongdoing yet still, in forgiveness, refuse to hate the wrongdoer, and indeed wish him well.

Something else that follows from the two-part conception of forgiveness is this: not only can the forgiver still hold the wrongdoer responsible for his actions, but she actually has to hold him responsible – if he isn't responsible, then he isn't to blame, in which case the hostile feelings she overcomes weren't justified in the first place, and no forgiveness is called for. Holding someone responsible for their wrongdoings isn't in itself a way of holding them in contempt or wishing them ill; on the contrary, refusing to hold them responsible can easily be a form of patronising condescension, in which the offender is regarded as not really morally advanced enough to be responsible for his misdeeds. The person who holds the offender to be fully responsible regards him at least in one sense as a moral equal: he's capable of being praised or blamed for his actions because they are in some deep sense his own. (That, indeed, is why forgiveness is possible and may be appropriate.) So forgiveness and responsibility go hand in hand, and forgiveness isn't and mustn't be a kind of excuse-making.

The third implication of the two-stage view of forgiveness is so substantial, and has so many ramifications, that it will need a section to itself. This is the implication for punishment that our view of forgiveness entails.

Forgiveness and punishment

It's often thought that forgiveness really amounts to mercy – that is, the waiving of punishment – and that forgiveness must rule out any calls for, or endorsement of, punishment for the wrongdoer. There is a very limited truth to this view: forgiveness does rule out one ground for punishment, the victim's desire to see the perpetrator suffer. If what you as a victim want is the wrongdoer's suffering for its own sake or to make you feel better (or, in the current cliché, to achieve closure), then yes, forgiveness does rule that out. If you relish the suffering of the wrongdoer, if you feel with satisfaction that he's getting just what's coming to him, then you surely haven't forgiven him. But there are other grounds for punishment, and some of them can certainly be endorsed by people who have genuinely forgiven. For a start, it might be necessary for the wrongdoer to be punished as a deterrent to others, and the forgiver might well accept this. If a student passes off another person's work as his own his teacher may get over her annoyance and forgive him quite easily, continue to wish him well and hope to find some way of helping him to become a better student, but she may also insist that he be punished for his cheating, perhaps by failing the course and having to repeat it, since plagiarism is a serious academic offence and it's important to discourage others from doing it. You can wish another person well, but think that it's even more important to discourage and deter others from committing the same crimes, especially since the wrongdoer does in virtue of his offences deserve to be punished.

Indeed, it's possible to forgive someone for the crime they've committed, but accept that even apart from considerations of deterrence, the demands of justice require them to undergo some form of punishment. That is, forgiveness needn't dismiss the demands of retributive justice. This is a view that some people find very hard to accept, perhaps because they feel that the retributive element in punishment really just amounts to revenge. And how, they ask, can a desire for revenge possibly go along with forgiveness? They're right, it can't. Revenge seeks the suffering of the wrongdoer for the satisfaction of the erstwhile victim. Whatever the rights and wrongs of revenge are, it clearly can't go along with forgiveness. Wanting someone to suffer because it will make you feel better just can't coexist with overcoming hostile attitudes to him and wishing him well.

But as we've already seen, retributive justice is not the same as revenge. The central idea in retributive justice is the idea of desert: that the punishment is, and should be, what the perpetrator deserves. This is a crucial element in our ideas about punishment; without it, there would be nothing to stop us from enforcing the most hideous punishments on people if doing so would deter others from becoming criminals. Even if we do think that punishment's main function is to deter others (and the offender himself, of course) we still need the idea of what the offender deserves by way of punishment to set limits on what the state may do to him in the name of justice. And if we think that justice demands that the offender be punished, then even a forgiving victim might accede to that demand, and endorse the offender's punishment, in the name of justice.

A forgiving victim might also believe that the offender, especially if he's still entirely unrepentant about his wrongdoings, might need to be punished if he's ever to see what's wrong with the way he's behaved. Wishing a person well might include hoping that he comes to see how terrible his behaviour has been, as a step on the road to coming to see what a decent life should really be like. Some people may need to be punished in order to learn that kind of thing. Wanting what's good for a person very often does include wanting him to lead a morally decent life. Think of how we bring up our children, and what we hope for them. We bring them up to be honest and considerate and fair to others, and we do this for their sakes, and not just for the sake of the community at large. Many of us believe that a life of fairness and kindness and generosity just is better for a person than a life full of cheating and harming other people, even if that way lies success and riches (although very often, of course, it doesn't). We want our children to experience the deep satisfaction of caring about and helping other people as well as themselves, because we think that will enrich their lives; we don't want them to bully and kick their way towards their goals without joining in the networks of love and friendship that give meaning to most people's lives. On this view, if an offender comes to see how dreadful his behaviour was, that can be part of his coming to see what a better life for himself might be like. And that in turn is something that, if he can act on it, will help to make his life go better. So if being punished is the only way he can be brought to a realization of the moral nature of what he's done, then punishment is something that a forgiving victim might want for him as part of wishing him well. (We should, however, note realistically that many of our institutions of punishment don't have this effect at all, more's the pity.

On the contrary, they often teach people to be worse. But that's a problem – a major one – in the theory and practice of punishment, and investigating that issue further would take us too far from our central topic here.)

It's true, of course, that offenders often don't deserve to be forgiven, and to that extent if they are forgiven they won't be getting what they deserve. But we don't generally believe that people should always and only get what they deserve. ("Use every man after his desert, and who would 'scape whipping?", as Shakespeare rightly points out). Most of us have had reason to be glad, at some point or other in our lives, that people don't always get what they strictly deserve. And even where justice does demand punishment, it doesn't demand ill will, so the demands of justice can be met, if that's what the situation morally requires, even where there is forgiveness.

For all of these reasons, forgiveness needn't rule out punishment for the offender. What it does rule out is punishing the offender just to please the victim, just to satisfy her desire for his suffering. That desire is something that the forgiver has to give up on when she chooses to forgive.

Further implications of forgiveness

What about reconciliation? Is there anything about the two-part conception of forgiveness – in which we have both to overcome hostility towards the offender, and also to wish him well – which commits the forgiver to reconcile with the offender? As we saw in Chapter 3, this can be a very difficult aspect of the aftermath of conflict, with some victims feeling that they can't forgive their erstwhile tormentors, yet also thinking that reconciliation is needed if anything like normal life is to be resumed, and others feeling that perhaps they might be able to manage forgiveness, but that reconciliation is too much, or too dangerous, to ask of them. However there's nothing in the account of forgiveness we're exploring that insists that forgiveness must involve reconciliation. Very often it will, where no bad consequences are to be expected, but sometimes it won't, when reconciliation might expose the victim to further hostilities. An abused woman may forgive her partner, but feel that it's unsafe to be fully reconciled with him. And just as reconciliation isn't a necessary feature of forgiveness, so forgiveness isn't necessary for reconciliation. People can decide to rub along with others even where there is a leaden residue of justified resentment from past offences, because the alternative in terms of continued conflict is worse. But this doesn't amount to forgiveness, because it needn't involve the overcoming of all hostile attitudes, or the adopting of goodwill towards the offender.

Of course, often forgiveness will in fact include reconciliation, and it normally includes an openness to the possibility of reconciliation, should other reasons against it eventually fall away. But as we've already seen, there may be some cases where even that openness to reconciliation isn't a necessary feature of forgiveness. There are some atrocities that leave a stain on the soul of the one who commits them, a stain that precludes full reconciliation, and that can't be washed away even by the powerful solvent of forgiveness.

Finally, there's one more feature of forgiveness that we should mention. On the two-stage account, forgiveness involves altering our feelings, which may not be something we can do at will, since notoriously our feelings aren't under our immediate control; we can't just choose to feel happy, for example, or elated or depressed or calm or agitated. So although we've been talking about *deciding* to forgive, this is a rather misleading way of putting things. We can't decide to forgive, right here and now, in the way that we can decide to donate some money to a charity, or join a political pressure group, or apologise to someone we've treated badly. Forgiveness isn't in the first instance a matter of how we behave, although it will normally have significant consequences for what the forgiver does. But primarily it's something inward, which requires a change in our feelings, and our feelings are not under our direct control. People struggle to forgive, sometimes throughout a lifetime, and may never succeed. (C. S. Lewis reports that he once tried to forgive someone for thirty years before he succeeded.) What we can do is *try* to forgive or, perhaps better, set ourselves to forgive. And there are things that we *can* choose to do, that *are* within our power: we can bite back the bitter words, we can refuse to dish the malicious dirt, we can suppress the demand for vengeance. Doing these things may, in time, help us to change our feelings. There is, unfortunately, no ironclad guarantee it will work – in some circumstances, all that biting back and suppressing may in fact make the feelings worse:

> I was angry with my friend
> I told my wrath, my wrath did end.
> I was angry with my foe,
> I told it not, my wrath did grow.
>
> (William Blake, *A Poison Tree*)

However there are techniques for changing one's emotions and even one's character, although no doubt they vary from person to person. (Here is where we may look to psychological research for help.) Success in making these changes may not be wholly in our power. But if forgiveness is what we should be aiming at, then both trying and succeeding will be admirable, in their different ways. We can admire the person who gives it their best shot, for the effort and determination they display. We can admire the person who succeeds, for their achievement, for having actually done what they set out to do.

Meeting the objections

How does this conception fare in dealing with the principal arguments against forgiveness? The first of these is the criticism of the therapeutic conception of forgiveness, on the grounds that it's an inadequate and often self-indulgent view. The defender of forgiveness can in fact just accept this claim, because she can accept that forgiveness may not be as therapeutic as is sometimes claimed, and in some cases it may even be less therapeutic than alternatives such as revenge or indifference. She can readily concede all this, because she can also agree that therapeutic efficacy isn't always the most important consideration in establishing how victims, and the rest of us, should respond to perpetrators. Indeed, a defender of forgiveness can agree that much of the cheap boosterism about forgiveness as therapy is as shallow as it is facile, and that forgiveness is often a difficult and laborious project that might take a lifetime to complete. There's nothing in the conception of forgiveness we're defending here that ties it to any therapeutic advantages at all, although it doesn't, of course, rule them out.

The second major objection to forgiveness is that it fails to take the offence seriously enough. But as we've seen, condoning the offence or excusing the offender aren't part of forgiveness at all; in fact, they're incompatible with it. If an offence is to be forgiven, it has to be recognized for what it is. Full recognition of what the offence involved, and of all the harm it caused, may of course make it harder to forgive the perpetrator, but if the offence is downplayed or whitewashed, then what's being forgiven is not the original offence, but rather a pale and sanitized version of it. Here ease of forgiveness is bought at the price of ignoring the real nature of the wrongdoing; it's a paradigm case of an objectionably cheap and facile response to wrongdoing, the kind of thing that brings forgiveness into disrepute. But again, there's nothing in the two-stage conception of forgiveness to support any diminishment of the offences that are the occasion of forgiveness. And on this conception, forgiveness needn't rule out indignation. So if we want to emphasize the need for an explicit rejection of atrocity, a public refusal to collude with it, and the bearing of witness to the iniquity of what has been done to the innocent, then all these are compatible with forgiveness as we understand it.

Third, we come to the question of respect, and to what is perhaps the most serious objection to forgiveness. Many people think that a readiness to forgive the perpetrator betokens a failure of self-respect on the part of the victim, or a failure in respect towards the victim if the forgiveness is being offered by third parties.

We need a brief digression here to deal with the question of third-party forgiveness. It's sometimes said that third-party forgiveness — that is, forgiveness by someone who isn't the primary victim — is either impossible or illegitimate. How can you forgive if you weren't the one who was harmed; and isn't it presumptuous in the extreme to suppose that you can do so? There's a kernel of truth in this view: certainly no one can forgive on behalf of the victim except the victim herself. But it does seem clear that third parties, who haven't themselves been harmed or wronged, can feel strong ill will towards offenders on account of their offences. People can hate and resent others on account of what those others have done to helpless innocents; think, for example, of the hostility often shown by anonymous members of the public towards those who have harmed children. But although they feel hatred and contempt and general ill will, the possibility exists that they might at some point overcome that ill will and adopt an attitude of at least minimal goodwill towards those whose offences have prompted such outrage. On the understanding of forgiveness that we're now working with, that just amounts to forgiving them. So third-party forgiveness is at least possible.

It's true that some people's linguistic intuitions tell them very strongly that you just can't call it forgiveness if it doesn't come from the victim. Perhaps what we can say in reply is that when a third party overcomes her contempt and ill will for a wrongdoer, then what's going on, morally speaking, is the same kind of thing as what happens when a victim overcomes her hatred and ill will for the person who wronged her. It matters less what we call this phenomenon than what it actually consists in; and the really pressing question here is whether this change in the attitude of third parties can be justified, or whether it amounts instead to some serious failure to respect the primary victims, the ones who did actually suffer the wrongdoing.

The parallel concern about first-party forgiveness — forgiveness by the victim herself — is the worry that a victim who is ready to forgive the offender is showing a lack of proper *self*-respect. Far from making a generous gesture, the forgiving victim is actually driven by too low an opinion of her own importance: a low opinion that is a sign not of admirable modesty, but instead of a pathetic subservience. Every offender displays a lack of respect for the victim, and the thought lying behind this objection to forgiveness is that resentment is an appropriate response, the *right* response, to the attack on one's standing that the original offence involves. So on this view, giving up on resentment implies accepting the low status that the wrongdoer assigns to the victim. The wrongdoer rates the victim as being so unimportant that it's fine to harm and wrong her, and the victim who forgives him is really assenting to that low opinion of her status; she's saying that yes, harming or wronging her doesn't really matter. But it does matter, say those who have this worry about forgiveness: no one should be so meek and subservient as to think that their being harmed or wronged is unimportant. This isn't modesty; it's a failure in proper self-respect.

Of course, such things are possible. Some people do lack sufficient self-respect, and their forgiveness is a kind of colluding with the offender's contempt for them. Indeed, Nietzsche's view is that the very resentment that people feel towards those who have wronged them is a sign of their weakness of character, and their overcoming of that resentment in forgiveness is further evidence of their low self-esteem and their desperate attempt to make themselves immune to the hostility or contempt of others. But although this may sometimes happen, it certainly isn't an inevitable feature of forgiveness. Nietzsche is conflating one possible mode of forgiveness with all possible versions of it. People's self-respect can have very different bases. It's true that for some, their self-respect is almost entirely derived from the opinion of others, and where those opinions are derogatory then that self-respect is indeed under attack. In such cases, it is indeed possible that forgiveness is a response to the threat to self-esteem made by the offender and his offence, and it may be a sign of a lack of self-respect.

But there are other ways of grounding self-respect. Self-respect can be based not on the opinions of others but on the recognition that all of us are worthy of respect for the individual persons that we are. Just as we should show respect to others, so they should show respect to us. Where offenders fail to do so, the fault is in them, not in their victims. This kind of self-respect isn't earned from or bestowed by others, and can't be lost by their failure to acknowledge it. Self-respect based on this ground isn't threatened by offenders, and overcoming resentment towards them displays no failure in it. Someone whose self-respect had this basis could still have resentment to overcome, since we can be hurt by, and resent, neglect or slights or malicious treatment by others, even where we are sure that this treatment was unjustified and where our self-respect isn't eroded by it. This resentment needs to be overcome for forgiveness to take place, but doing so needn't involve any objectionable servility, or failure in self-respect.

All offences that wrong someone do involve a failure to treat them with sufficient respect. But forgiveness needn't imply any acceptance of the verdict (implicit or explicit) in that failure. Abandoning ill will and adopting goodwill doesn't mean accepting the views or the verdicts or the values of the offender whom you're choosing to forgive. Silence about the wrongfulness of the offence doesn't imply consent or endorsement of the disrespect implicit in it, and in any case forgiveness needn't be silent – it can go hand-in-hand with strong protest. What seems to be at the heart of the self-respect objection to forgiveness is the assumption that forgiveness involves some kind of *concession* to the offender's view of the matter. But this assumption is a mistake: forgiveness is better seen as a gift, not a concession, and a gift can be given freely to people whose attitudes you nonetheless reject. What we're trying to find out is whether forgiveness need involve any failure in respect to the victim; simply assuming that forgiveness makes a concession to the view that the victim needn't be respected begs the question at issue.

Is this forgiveness?

At this point, however, a quite new and different problem may emerge. Is what we're talking about still recognizably a conception of *forgiveness*? We're trying to show that this account can meet the strong objections to forgiveness that have been levelled at it, but does this conception have enough in common with our ordinary understanding of forgiveness to count as the same kind of thing at all? Does it really amount to forgiveness? We've been arguing that forgiveness is compatible with the maintenance of anger and indignation; also, in some cases, with the demand that the perpetrator be punished in full for his crimes; even, in some circumstances, with the refusal to re-establish prior good relations. But is the situation of a person who has been forgiven in this way any different from that of someone who hasn't been forgiven at all? Is forgiveness really what's going on here?

Suppose that both you and I have been kidnapped and held hostage by a third person: Adolphus, let's call him. During our captivity we're treated very badly indeed, with frequent beatings, and we're in constant fear for our lives. But now we've escaped, and Adolphus has been arrested and charged with these offences. You announce that what he did was unforgivable, that his brutality and selfishness were appalling (which indeed they were) and the kind of thing that must be publicly denounced, that Adolphus deserves to spend many years in jail, and that you'll do your best to see that he does. Above all, you declare, there's no question of you forgiving him, since he certainly doesn't deserve it. I, on the other hand, decide to forgive Adolphus. But I also point out, perhaps in the national press, that what he did was brutal and selfish, that it's important that everyone realizes that that kind of behaviour is appalling (which indeed it is); furthermore, for reasons of deterrence and retribution it's important that Adolphus be punished, and so I'm ready to testify against him in the witness box at his trial. Still, I do forgive him, I insist: I've overcome my (entirely justified) resentment of his vile behaviour, and I wish him well. Indeed, I hope that his years in jail will help him to understand the wrongness of what he's done, and to become a better person, because that way his life will go better.

Have I really forgiven Adolphus? On the conception we're trying to defend here I surely have, since I've overcome resentment and adopted goodwill towards him. But my actual behaviour towards him is barely distinguishable from that of someone who definitely hasn't forgiven him at all. Surely, it might be said, the conception of forgiveness we're using here is just too remote from the more ordinary understanding of forgiveness, which sees it as an attitude that involves saying that the offence didn't really matter, or agreeing to wipe the slate clean, or forgetting all about it. Surely an attitude that remains indignant about the offence and acknowledges the need to punish the offender just can't count as the same kind of thing; it isn't really forgiveness at all.

It's true that there is a range of different conceptions of forgiveness, and the one we're defending here is certainly at the more robust and unsentimental end of the spectrum. It contrasts very markedly with conceptions of forgiveness that involve putting the past entirely behind us, and moving onwards and upwards in therapeutic reconciliation. However, there are two features that tie our account tightly to the common core conception of forgiveness. First, on the two-part account forgiveness comes out as being *difficult,* since it calls for a full grasp of the violation of the moral order that the perpetrator has committed, and the overcoming of the resentment this naturally and justifiably produces. This difficulty in getting oneself to forgive is acknowledged in much of the literature on forgiveness, and is an immediately recognizable part of our common moral experience. Most of us know how hard it is to forgive someone who has harmed us, that it needs constant effort, and that although we may have thought we've forgiven the perpetrator we find again and again that feelings of rancour and contempt rise up in us towards him, so that the work of forgiveness still remains to be done. The robust conception of forgiveness certainly captures that aspect of it.

Second, a central element of our account is the overcoming of ill will, and the re-establishing of at least a modicum of goodwill towards the forgiven person. The difference between ill will and even a modest degree of goodwill is enormous, a difference in kind, as anyone who has faced a serious case of the former can testify. Indeed anyone who has felt ill will towards someone, and who then has changed that ill will to goodwill – perhaps by forgiving them, or perhaps just by coming to see them in a new light – will know how profound the difference is, and how much it both results from and results in seeing the person differently. A conception of forgiveness that has that difference at its heart is not one in which forgiveness is negligible or invisible. But nor is it one that lends itself to the easy reconciliations and cheap boosterism rightly condemned by the case against forgiveness, which have diluted the general understanding both of what forgiveness really requires, and of the right response to violations of the moral order.

To sum up: forgiveness is different from condoning or excusing or wiping the slate clean. It has two principal elements: overcoming all hostile feelings towards the wrongdoer, and coming to wish him well. Forgiveness requires us to hold the wrongdoer responsible for his offences; it's compatible with indignation about what the wrongdoer has done; and it's compatible with endorsing punishment for him for deterrent or retributive reasons, although not for personal satisfaction at his suffering. Reconciliation is not a necessary aspect of forgiveness (and forgiveness isn't necessary for reconciliation either). Since forgiveness involves an inner change in the attitudes of the forgiver, this isn't something we can always choose to do at will, although we can choose to *try* to do it, and if we persist, we often succeed. This conception of forgiveness can meet the main objections to it, since it doesn't view forgiveness as primarily therapeutic, nor does it downplay the seriousness of the offence, nor involve any failure of respect for the victim. It's a robust conception of forgiveness in comparison to some others, but it shares the core elements of our ordinary idea of forgiveness: that it's difficult to do, and that it ultimately involves goodwill rather than ill will towards the wrongdoer.

We've argued that there's a conception of forgiveness – a genuine conception, in clear possession of the central elements of our ordinary usage of the term – which can meet the principal arguments that have been levelled against forgiveness. But this isn't by itself sufficient to demonstrate that forgiveness is the best response to wrongdoing. The case against forgiveness claims, rightly, that resentment and refusal to forgive are often warranted: they're justified by what the offender did; they're a legitimate response to the cruelty or meanness or malice of the wrongdoing that elicits them; they're what the wrongdoer *deserves*. So why should we prefer to forgive? To answer that question, it won't be enough to show that there aren't any conclusive arguments against forgiveness, given that the maintenance of hostility is often so clearly an appropriate response to wrongdoing. If we want to show that forgiveness is preferable, we need to find some positive arguments in its favour. We need also to address the issue raised by Améry's and Lomax's differing stances: the question of whether forgiveness should always be conditional on repentance, or whether the positive arguments also apply to unconditional forgiveness. These will be the tasks of the final chapter of this book.

6. The case for forgiveness III: the positive arguments

I declared myself ready to forgive my enemies, and perhaps even to love them, but only when they showed certain signs of repentance, that is, when they ceased being enemies. In the opposite case, that of the enemy who remains an enemy, who perseveres in his desire to inflict suffering, it is certain that one must not forgive him: one can try to salvage him, one can (one must!) discuss with him, but it is our duty to judge him, not to forgive him. (Levi 1986: 222–3)

Everyone says forgiveness is a lovely idea, until they have something to forgive, as we had during the war. ... And half of you already want to ask me, "I wonder how you'd feel about forgiving the Gestapo if you were a Pole or a Jew?" So do I. I wonder very much. ... When you start mathematics you do not begin with the calculus; you begin with simple addition. In the same way, if we really want (but it all depends on really wanting) to learn how to forgive, perhaps we had better start with something easier than the Gestapo. One might start with forgiving one's husband or wife, or the nearest NCO, for something they have done or said in the last week. That will probably keep us busy for the moment. (Lewis 1952: 101–2)

Sometime the hating has to stop. (Lomax 1995: 276)

We've seen that the main objections to forgiveness can be met, if we have a suitably robust conception of forgiveness. But the case against forgiveness is far too strong to be dismissed out of hand. Victims do have a right to resent those who have wronged them, and in the case of serious offences, they also have a right to hate. But rights are the kind of thing that can be waived by the rights-bearer: I have a right to my own property, but can waive it if I choose to give some of it away. Victims can waive their right to resentment and hatred, but what we need to find out is whether they have any positive reason to do so. Even if the victim has good reason to maintain resentment against the offender, it doesn't follow that there can be no other reasons that overcome that one; it's possible that a legitimate reason for resentment may nonetheless be legitimately outweighed. So what positive reasons can be offered for overcoming resentment and forgiving the perpetrator? There are two principal candidates in answer to this question: respect for persons and human solidarity.

Respect for persons

The first of these views says that each of us, including each wrongdoer, is a unique individual, a person of inestimable value, and it's out of respect for their personhood that we should overcome hostility to wrongdoers and offer them goodwill. However, promising though this looks, further scrutiny suggests that respect for persons doesn't in fact produce a reason for forgiving offenders that stands up to close examination.

We're told that we should forgive wrongdoers out of recognition of, and respect for, the fact that they're persons. It's certainly true that we should treat persons as persons, and not as lesser creatures, and we should respect their ability to choose for themselves. There are some things, such as torture, that we shouldn't do to anyone, just out of respect for the fact that they're a person. But the resentment that is justified by the actions of wrongdoers, and which would have to be overcome in forgiving them, is something we only offer to persons anyway. We don't resent a hurricane, or a ferocious animal, nor do we feel contempt for it: we know that it doesn't understand the nature of what it's doing, or the harm it's inflicting on us. We may dislike it, or even hate it, but it would be pointless to *resent* a dangerous animal, to think that it *ought* to have done otherwise, unless we really believed that it understood morality and could choose for itself. However, when we resent human beings who have knowingly harmed us, it's precisely because we do recognize that they're persons who have the ability to choose for themselves. Admittedly we don't recognize them as being persons in good standing, but how could we, in the light of what they've done? All the same, the resentment and contempt we feel for them are just as much recognition of, and responses to, personhood as forgiveness is. So the fact that we ought to respect persons doesn't seem to produce any more reason to forgive than it does to resent.

The characteristics that distinguish persons from animals include such things as the ability to reason, and an understanding of right and wrong. But in the case of serious offenders at least, the use to which they've put these distinctive characteristics has been so distorted and degraded that it's hard to see why respect for them as persons should lead to any remission in ill will. We can't respect what they've done with their personal capacities; and we acknowledge that they have these capacities just as much when we resent them as when we forgive them. Indeed, we could quite reasonably say that we respect their personhood precisely in holding them responsible for their actions, in blaming them for their wrongdoings and in resenting their choice to harm or wrong us. We don't, after all, offer any of these responses to creatures that aren't persons. Usually we kill animals that are inconvenient to us out of hand, and the fact that we don't do that with human offenders

– the fact that extra-judicial murder is prohibited – is already a mark of our respect for their personhood. Why would respect for persons mean that we should also forgive them? An extra argument is needed to show us that: the mere fact that they're persons isn't by itself enough. And it's hard to see what that extra argument might be.

Human solidarity

A different and better alternative as a reason to forgive wrongdoers derives from the facts of our common human nature. Here the focus is on our shared humanity, and hence our shared human frailty and fallibility. Most people, by the time they're adults, know something about their own capacities for wrongdoing; most of us are aware that even in fairly benign and supportive circumstances, we don't do everything we ought to. Very few of us can honestly say to ourselves that we've done everything we should, and nothing that we shouldn't, even in the last twenty-four hours. For many of us, believers and unbelievers alike, one of the parts of the New Testament that speaks most vividly to our condition is St Paul saying, "The good that I would I do not, and the evil that I would not, that I do." Ovid said something very similar a little earlier: "I see and approve the better, and do the worse". And several hundred years before that, Plato remarked that each one of us is like a charioteer, with two headstrong horses pulling in different directions. Our divided nature has been noticed since we began to notice anything much about ourselves. And in unpropitious circumstances this can lead beyond the ordinary wrongdoing that most of us have an intimate knowledge of, to something altogether more terrible. The history of the human race shows again and again with dreadful clarity that more of us than we would like to think are capable of enacting horrific atrocities.

Our common human nature contains much that is good, of course, or we wouldn't individually or collectively have survived to be discussing it today. But it also contains a very dark element, which we can recognize in ourselves as well as in others. In the case of the worst horrors, let's hope that it's true to say that we wouldn't have done what the perpetrators of them did; but it's not unreasonable to think that in certain circumstances some of us who are currently living relatively blameless lives could also have done terrible things. There are famous experiments in psychology that seem to show that perfectly ordinary people are prepared to inflict considerable suffering on others if they're told to do so by a person in authority, or even simply permitted to do so by authority figures. The most notable of these experiments were conducted by Stanley Milgram in Connecticut in the 1960s:

Volunteers for a psychology experiment were told that they were taking part in a study on the effects of learning. When the "learner" gave a wrong answer, each participant was ordered to press a switch, having been told that this would give the "learner" an electric shock. The "learner" was attached to an electrode and strapped to a chair in the next room. (In fact there were no electric shocks and the "learner" was only acting the part.) Participants were made to think that, by pressing different switches, they were giving increasingly severe shocks, and the "learner" acted as if this were so.

There were 30 switches, ranging from 15 to 430 volts. At 75 volts the "learner" grunted. At 120 volts he protested. At 150 he demanded to be released from the experiment. As the voltage increased, the protests rose, reaching an agonised scream at 285 volts. Participants who hesitated were ordered to continue. Those asking for guidance were advised to continue after a brief pause. After the 315-volt "shock", the victim kicked on the wall again, but the participant was ordered to continue right up to the maximum of 450 volts. To reach this apparent voltage, it was necessary to pull the switch through positions marked slight shock/moderate shock/strong shock/very strong shock/intense shock/extreme intensity shock/danger: severe shock/XXX 450 volts. Of the 40 participants, 26 continued all the way to the last shock on the generator. A number showed obvious signs of stress, suggesting they really did believe they were obeying orders to inflict severe pain.   (Glover 1999: 332)

One of the most significant features of the Milgram experiments was that they were conducted on people who weren't brought up in a particularly authoritarian way, nor had they lived in an especially obedient and deferential society. One implication is that it's a wide-spread feature of human nature to obey authority even when it's issuing appalling orders; another even darker implication may be that it's part of human nature to be ready to inflict terrible suffering on others, and that this aspect of our nature can be easily released into action when authority provides a ready excuse.

It's true that some of the volunteers in Milgram's experiments refused to inflict what they believed to be agonising electric shocks on an innocent human being. But about two-thirds of them didn't refuse (and these proportions have been replicated in other experiments). Few of us can say with absolute confidence that we ourselves would have refused. The implications for our possible complicity in genuinely terrible actions are not exactly reassuring. And even where we can truly say that the persons who we are now simply couldn't act as the worst perpetrators did, it may still be true that had our early circumstances been different, we might have turned into the kind of people who could have carried out those atrocities. As Primo Levi, who survived Auschwitz, pointed out, many of the people who did carry out those atrocities were not monsters: they were human beings like you and me. Another way to put this thought is that if they are monsters, then so potentially are we: there's a recurring streak of evil in the human blueprint.

This isn't to provide any kind of excuse or condoning of what wrongdoers have done. "There but for the grace of God go I" only sounds like an excuse if we suppose that anything that I myself could do can't be so very bad after all. But only a monstrous egoist could possibly believe this. In recognizing that I too could have acted as the perpetrators did, I'm recognizing that I too could be fully responsible for terrible wrongdoing, and hence a fit object for resentment and hatred.

We are not here suggesting, and do most strongly not believe, that this involves any moral equivalence between the perpetrator and the victim. Responsibility belongs to those who perpetrate the wrongs; their victims are in this respect innocent. However, knowledge about what we ourselves might have done in the perpetrator's circumstances can properly affect the attitudes we take to these truths about the perpetrator's responsibility; it can make a difference to whether we see them as totally alien beings sharing nothing in common with us, or whether we recognize, perhaps with horror, our common humanity in them. Awareness of our own moral frailty and susceptibility to wrongdoing increases our sense of commonality with all who share the human predicament and its terrible possibilities. And out of that dreadful commonality, a reason for forgiveness may emerge.

Before we come to that reason, though, we should look at an alternative view. Some people think that these facts about human moral frailty justify the view that a regime of harsh punishments, with explicit refusals to forgive, is what's needed to keep us all on the straight and narrow. In their view, it's precisely because we do have these dreadful possibilities within us that we need to set our faces publicly and uncompromisingly against those who give free rein to their darkest motivations. Anything more indulgent than that, they say, encourages and colludes with the evil that's in us.

Forgiveness is a sentimental luxury that's inadequate to the realities of the situation, and it's one the perpetrators certainly don't deserve.

This is to treat the question of forgiveness as primarily a matter of producing the best consequences. But that's too narrow and impoverished a view of what's at stake here. Just as there's more to the justification of forgiveness than its supposed therapeutic effects for the individual victim, so there's more to it than its supposed beneficial effects for society at large. What we're trying to decide is what is the fitting, the appropriate, the *right* attitude to take to our fellow humans who have behaved in such terrible ways, and this isn't exclusively a question of how to deter them and others from doing so again.

In any case we don't actually know whether a commitment to forgiveness or a policy of unremitting hostility to wrongdoers will in fact produce the best results with respect to future wrongdoing. We do have reason to believe, however, that nothing at all – not universal forgiveness nor the greatest hostility nor the most stringent punishments – will keep all of us or even most of us permanently on the straight and narrow. Whatever policy we adopt to deter perpetrators, the question will still arise of what attitude we should take to them when deterrence has failed. And with respect to deterrence, then as we have seen forgiveness is compatible with the demand for punishment, hence punishment's deterrent power is still available to those who endorse forgiveness. So the unforgiving response to our common moral weakness isn't necessarily the best one; there's still room for us to consider what reasons there might be to forgive.

In what way, then, does our common human frailty provide a reason for forgiveness? We could, of course, just write off the perpetrators of terrible wrongdoing, since hate is not an unreasonable response to what they have done. But given our common human nature, this will be a verdict on our own possible selves as well as on them: we'll be saying that we also should be written off if we become like them. It's hard to want this for ourselves should that possibility become a terrible actuality. And there is an alternative: an awareness of our common humanity, our recognition of commonality with the worst of human beings as well as with the best, may produce in us a sense of solidarity with them just as members of the human race – a feeling that like it or not, we're all in this together, and we all have some affiliation with and responsibility for each other. This solidarity is not, of course, with the perpetrators' terrible actions, but rather with them as human beings, however twisted and distorted they have become. Even the worst of wrongdoers, on this view, is still one of us; he's part of the human family, and we have a stake in his future, for good or ill.

For those who doubt the existence of a general sense of solidarity with the human race, it's worth pointing out that although it's often very tenuous, it's surprisingly evident in certain circumstances. Many charities depend on it for the donations that are their life-blood; they show us people we've never met, living in faraway countries we've never visited, and we recognize their needs as having some claim on us, because each one of them is also one of us, one of the human race. Another indication of our sense of human solidarity arises when we see or hear of some splendid human achievement or act of generosity towards others. "It makes you proud to be human" is what we sometimes say. Similarly, when we hear of some ghastly atrocity the description of which sickens the air we breathe, we sometimes say, "You feel ashamed to be human when you hear of that kind of thing." These responses are evidence of a sense of connectedness, however weak, between all of us as co-members of the same species, who share the same human predicament. It's analogous to, although very much weaker than, our sense of connectedness with members of our family. They too sometimes behave very badly indeed, but we have a reason to forgive them when they do, just because they're "one of us".

Similarly our sense of common humanity, our awareness that we too as members of the human family could be offenders and in need of forgiveness, whether or not we were to realize it at the time, gives us a reason to forgive those members who have actually become offenders, who have failed to meet the moral demands of the human condition under which we all labour. It's a reason of reciprocity: because we could be, or could have been, in their position, and in need of solidarity and forgiveness, so we have reason to forgive those who really are in that position. We're not actually obliged to do so, just as we're not obliged to hope for forgiveness from others should we too become wrongdoers. But it's permissible to do so: nothing in the legitimacy of resentment against offenders makes it obligatory to retain that resentment. We can, if we choose, give it up. (It may be obligatory to retain the demand for justice but, as we've already seen, forgiveness is compatible with maintaining that demand.)

This kind of solidarity does not, of course, take precedence over solidarity with the victims; that's always more important, precisely because being victims they deserve our support, whereas the perpetrators do not. Nevertheless solidarity with the victims, and recognition of our commonality with them in their innocent vulnerability, doesn't by itself preclude a different although much more troubling solidarity with perpetrators, and recognition of our common moral frailty and susceptibility to degradation. This solidarity must coexist with the maintenance of total moral rejection of what the perpetrators have done; otherwise it descends into collusion with them. We must hate and reject the atrocity, but we don't have to hate the perpetrators of it. Maintaining that dual stance, although difficult, isn't impossible, and where it exists we can see that there is a reason to forgive even the worst perpetrators, and to hope for their future improvement. They are, after all, one of us.

There are of course different kinds of solidarity, and thoughts about solidarity as a reason for forgiveness can kick in at different levels, so to speak. My reason for forgiveness in a particular case may be quite specific to that case; I may forgive a particularly tiresome and difficult person because she is, after all, my sister (and she may forgive me for similar reasons, too). The fact that she's family is doing a lot of the work here: it's a kind of very local solidarity. But as we have seen, a more general solidarity is also available as a reason for forgiveness: the solidarity we can feel for all of us who find ourselves in the human condition, burdened with our flawed and faulty human nature. And that broader solidarity can itself be seen as an example of an even more general reason for forgiveness: a wider worldview involving a commitment to love (and its cognates, such as goodwill) rather than hate (and its cognates of ill will and malice). Even where hate is entirely legitimate, we may prefer to choose love. Such preferences are basic, and cannot be further defended. But many people share this one, at least in principle. Even Jeffrie Murphy, who defends resentment so persuasively in his book *Getting Even*, thinks that in the end all of us would prefer to be inscribed in the Book of Love rather than in the Book of Hate, and that's a preference that may give us reason to choose forgiveness over even a fully justified, entirely legitimate resentment.

There's one further issue about forgiveness to be addressed: the question of whether forgiveness should be conditional on repentance, or whether unconditional forgiveness, offered even to unrepentant wrongdoers, is also morally legitimate. Many people, perhaps a majority of those who endorse forgiveness at all, think that we should only forgive those who show clear remorse. They think that we really have no reason to forgive someone who is untroubled by his own misdeeds or crimes, who would commit them again if he got half a chance, and whose only regrets are about getting caught, or even about how few wrongs he managed to commit. One such case was the Rwandan killer who, after the genocide there had been brought to an end, whispered to one of his surviving victims that he really should have killed her too. There were unrepentant

Nazis as well, who after the end of the war regretted only the loss of their power and the demise of the Third Reich. Do we have any reason at all to forgive people in so horrific, so degraded a moral condition?

It's certainly a lot easier to see why we might have reason to forgive a repentant wrongdoer. In showing remorse, in repenting of his deeds, the wrongdoer now aligns himself with the victim, and no longer stands in deadly opposition to her. He now shares her view of the nature of the offence and her condemnation of it, and this makes it much easier to overcome resentment and hatred towards him. It's also easier to wish him well, since he himself has started on the road to becoming a better person than he was when he committed the offences. Survivors of great atrocities such as Primo Levi and Jean Améry felt that remorse and repentance was a necessary condition of forgiveness: that without it forgiveness would be wrong and should not be contemplated. Eric Lomax, who suffered the terrible after-effects of torture, both physical and psychological, for forty years after his experiences in the Japanese prisoner-of-war camp, finally forgave his torturer, and felt great release at doing so; but the man he forgave was as repentant as it is possible to be, and had devoted the rest of his life, through all those long years of Lomax's suffering, to trying to make amends for the horrors he had engaged in during the war. There's no reason to think that Lomax would have wanted to forgive him, or indeed would have felt able to, without that total repentance.

Nonetheless, the question still remains: do we have any reason to forgive even unrepentant wrongdoers? If we base forgiveness on solidarity, or more broadly on the preferability of love over hate, then there seems to be no way of denying that we do have such a reason. The unrepentant perpetrator is still one of us; we can still think, in the worst cases with horror, that we too could have been in his condition, feeling his appalling and degraded self-satisfaction at the contemplation of his terrible activities. Difficult though it undoubtedly would be, we can still overcome ill will and wish him well, although that would in his case amount to hoping that somehow, somewhere, he might come to see the moral truth of his atrocity, as the first step on the road to becoming a better person. That is what Améry hoped against hope that the withholding of forgiveness and the maintaining of resentment might do, and his hope was an entirely legitimate one. With or without forgiveness, though, it's often a very forlorn hope indeed. But it's a hope that the forgiver can share.

The value of forgiveness

We've spent a lot of time in this book considering whether forgiveness is always permissible, or whether it's sometimes just wrong, ruled out by other moral considerations. We've argued that it is indeed always permissible, that since forgiveness can meet the principal criticisms against it, it's never actually wrong to forgive. But it doesn't follow that all cases of forgiveness are admirable. Here as elsewhere, people can do the right thing for the wrong reasons. As we've seen, forgiveness can be proffered for a variety of self-serving and discreditable reasons. In fact where such motives predominate it often isn't clear that forgiveness – the overcoming of ill will and the adoption of at least minimal goodwill – has actually taken place. If the desired outcome – the recognition by others of one's own occupation of the moral high ground, the keeping of the peace, or the warm glow of self-admiration – fails to materialize, an uprush of resentment often reveals that the work of forgiveness is still to be done. But even where forgiveness has actually taken place, it often remains shallow and facile, having been undertaken for such self-regarding considerations. Nonetheless, in all such cases the possibility will remain of a forgiveness undertaken for good reasons, difficult though this will generally be.

The case against forgiveness derives much of its strength from the fact that there's more than enough evil in the world to generate good reasons to hate its perpetrators. If forgiveness is a gift, above and beyond the call of duty, then it follows that many cases of resentment and hatred are not morally blameworthy. More than that: they may be morally preferable to those cases of facile forgiveness where the actual motives for forgiving are shallow and discreditable. The sustained resentment of a Jean Améry may be of far greater moral worth than the cheap forgiveness of a Uriah Heep. Nonetheless, so we have argued, there are always reasons available to us which tell in favour of forgiveness, reasons stemming from human solidarity, from a consciousness of our common moral frailty and susceptibility to evil, and from a commitment to the value of goodwill, and more broadly of love.

However, arguing that forgiveness is always *permissible*, that it isn't actually wrong to forgive, is hardly offering a very ringing endorsement. Most attitudes and activities that are permissible aren't especially admirable: it isn't wrong to learn how to scuba dive, but there needn't be anything especially admirable about it. But right at the beginning of the book we suggested that it's *admirable* to forgive, that the capacity for forgiveness is a virtue, and we need to try to make good on this claim. In fact, although there is indeed something that can be said about this, it's surprisingly short, and it doesn't really consist in argument at all. Forgiveness is admirable because it represents a moral achievement: the triumph of goodwill over ill will, of love over hate. Of course, some people don't accept that love is better than hate, or that it's always better than hate. But we can't really argue for that claim, because here we've reached moral bedrock. We don't know of any more fundamental thought we could appeal to in order to back it up. In some ways this is similar to the impossibility of arguing in support of the basic laws of logic. How could we argue for the claim that we shouldn't contradict ourselves? It isn't possible, because noncontradiction is basic to all argument whatsoever, and there's nothing else to appeal to. Things are rather similar in the sphere of basic moral values: we can't actually *argue* that love is better than hate, because there's nothing else more fundamental to appeal to. All we can do is to give examples of heroic forgiveness, such as that of Gordon Wilson, or Eric Lomax, and then invite people to consider what love is like, and what hate is like; and in the light of that consideration, to see whether they share our intuitions about such cases.

Suppose we're right about love being better than hate. Does that mean that we ought to forgive, that we have a *duty* to do so? In some cases, we really do have such a duty. If the offence was a relatively small one, and if the offender has apologised and made amends, then we'd be wrong to refuse to forgive. But in other, more serious cases, or where the wrongdoer shows no remorse at all, we're surely not obliged to forgive him; we don't actually have a duty to forgive. Here, forgiveness is a free gift, and we can't be required to give it. It's true that some gifts, like those we give at Christmas, are ones that we are expected to give. Not giving any Christmas presents to family and friends would be seen, probably correctly, as mean and stingy. But we don't think that the gift of forgiveness in these serious cases is like that. Part of its attractiveness lies in the very fact that it is freely given. No one could *demand* that Gordon Wilson forgive the terrorists who murdered his daughter, or that Eric Lomax forgive the man who tortured him.

But now this may seem puzzling. For if forgiveness, when it's given in the right way and in the right spirit, is the best response to wrongdoing, the one that's most admirable, isn't that the response we really ought to make? And, if we don't forgive, aren't we open to criticism? But in discussing the Truth and Reconciliation Commission, we resolutely set our face against any suggestion that refusing to forgive is a failure, or that those who continue to resent are morally inferior in some way. But if it's really better to forgive, why can't it be morally demanded of people? Why shouldn't we tell the victims that really, all things considered, they *ought* to forgive their tormentors?

The mere thought of making any such moral demand of the victims of atrocities should make anyone contemplating it cringe. But we do need an explanation of why this is the case.

People do many heroic and saintly things that no one thinks we have any right to demand of them. They risk their lives to rescue people from burning buildings; they give organs to strangers to save them from fatal diseases; they hide the victims of murderous oppression, at enormous risk to themselves. And we greatly admire such deeds. But, given what it costs, or could cost, the person who does them, we aren't justified either in demanding that they do such things, or in looking down on them in any way at all if they don't. What we can demand from people (including ourselves) is morally decent behaviour, and that's hard enough for most of us; but the hero and the saint go far beyond this. We look up to them; we recognize that they're morally better than most of us, but we don't think that they have a duty to be like that, or that others should be subject to criticism because they are not. Forgiveness, especially of great wrongs committed by a perpetrator who feels no remorse for what he's done, is in this category: those who can manage it are admirable, they're better than most of us, but they don't actually have a duty to do it. Indeed, that's part of what's so admirable about them: the forgiveness they offer to the wrongdoer is way beyond the demands of duty. It is indeed a free gift.

It might still be argued that if love is a *morally* better response than hate, that means we have more reason to forgive than not, even if forgiveness isn't something others can demand of us. But if that's true, then surely the person who refuses to forgive is failing to do what he has most reason to do? And isn't failing to do what you've got most reason to do something for which you can rightly be criticized?

Persuasive though this argument initially sounds, it isn't ultimately convincing. Even if forgiveness is more morally admirable than the refusal to forgive, it doesn't follow that there is actually more reason to forgive. For, as we've seen, there are powerful reasons for not forgiving, and those reasons may in some cases be just as strong as the ones there are to forgive. Consider the person who's prepared to donate one of his kidneys to save his sister's life, but when he goes into hospital for a tissue test he discovers that he isn't a match for his sister, and so he can't donate his kidney to her. Her body would reject the alien tissue. However, he also discovers that he's a match for someone else who needs a kidney: someone totally unknown and unrelated to him. In this situation, there are very good reasons to donate and very good reasons not to. It seems clear that if he decides to donate and transforms this stranger's life, he has done something morally splendid. But it doesn't follow that if he decides not to go through this painful and risky procedure that he was acting on reasons that are any the less strong. If he refuses, he does so for perfectly proper reasons: the procedure is painful and risky, and the person is a stranger. However, although his refusal would be completely *justified* and it would be quite wrong to criticize his decision in any way, still, his decision doesn't particularly call for *admiration*. It can perfectly well be endorsed, but on other grounds. We can *respect* his decision, and think it perfectly *proper* and wholly *rational*. Similar things can be said about those who forgive, and those who do not. People who forgive the unrepentant, or those who have committed a terrible wrong against them, do something tremendously difficult, courageous and generous. But those who don't are perfectly justified in their refusal, and act on reasons that are, at least sometimes, just as strong.

In fact, we can go one step further. There may be cases, there very probably *are* cases, when the refusal to forgive is also admirable. If a person is under strong and illegitimate pressure to forgive a wrongdoer, perhaps because it's convenient for others to sweep the whole wrongful incident under the carpet, and if he refuses to yield to this pressure and insists on maintaining his genuine resentment at the injustice of what was done, then that too may be admirable. Indeed, in some situations it may be that only people who maintain a strong and bitter resentment have the psychological energy to go on fighting for the recognition of injustice, and for a better response to it than facile forgiveness. In such a situation, the person who refuses to forgive can be doing something admirable, and we shouldn't ignore this possibility, even though the person who offers a genuine forgiveness, and also continues to fight for justice, may be doing something even better. None of this should really surprise us, since the moral world we live in is a complicated place, and conflicting actions may sometimes both be good. The person who goes halfway around the world to help strangers who are in desperate need of her medical skills does something admirable; the person who stays at home to look after his ailing parents and disabled sibling also does something admirable. So it sometimes is with forgiveness and its converse.

We started this enquiry by asking whether forgiveness was always the right thing to do. We've seen that the case against forgiveness is a very strong one; that some forms of forgiveness are cheap and facile; and that victims have a right to feel resentment and sometimes hatred for those who have so desperately harmed them. We've argued that there is a robust conception of forgiveness that can meet the criticisms contained in the case against it, and that there are positive reasons, of solidarity and of a commitment to love in preference to hate, for forgiving perpetrators rather than maintaining hostility towards them. These reasons apply to unrepentant as well as to repentant wrongdoers, and so we have a justification for unconditional forgiveness. However, none of these reasons amount to a duty or obligation to forgive; it remains an unforced gift, and it also remains true that victims have reasons, sometimes just as strong, to maintain resentment towards those who have harmed them. Although there may be equally strong reasons for resentment as for forgiveness, forgiveness is more admirable because it goes beyond the call of duty, because of its difficulty and its generosity and because, in the end, love is preferable to hate. However the maintenance of resentment, where it's put at the service of bringing about justice, can also be an admirable thing to do.

Forgiveness is hard. It has forms that are morally negligible or worse. But at its highest, it shows solidarity with our fellow humans; not when they're at their magnificent best, but when they're at their worst, tainted with evil and low in the dust. It's a strike in favour of love, for the worst of us as well as for the best: that is, for what any one of us might, or might have, become. The needs of victims, and solidarity with them, are always more important than solidarity with perpetrators. Nevertheless, we still have to decide what attitude to take to wrongdoers. Choosing to forgive them acknowledges the nature of what they've done, terrible as it sometimes is, but also remains open to hope for something better in the future: a hope that is often utterly disappointed, but which nonetheless returns again and again.

Further reading

We naturally hope that you will want to explore some of the issues in this book in greater depth. There is a vast amount written on the topic of forgiveness. The list that follows includes every piece we mentioned in the book and a few other pieces we have found helpful. Even so, the list is fairly formidable, so a few remarks about how to go on from here might be welcome.

If you are interested in differing views about forgiveness in the various world religions, we would recommend Mark Rye *et al.*, "Religious Perspectives on Forgiveness" (2001) as a starting place. Anthony Bash's excellent book *Forgiveness and Christian Ethics* (2007) not only explores Christian approaches to forgiveness, but also gives a general critical survey of the arguments and literature on the topic. Bishop Butler (an Anglican Bishop in the eighteenth century) famously discusses resentment and forgiveness in Sermons 8 and 9 of his *Fifteen Sermons*, of which there are many editions. The best short summary of the Christian view of forgiveness, and one that has influenced us in various ways, is to be found in the chapter with that title in C. S. Lewis's *Mere Christianity* (1952).

James Bowman's book on honour, *Honor: A History* (2006), helps to remind us of a tradition that shaped a lot of our thinking, but that has tended to drop out of sight a little in recent years, at least in the West, and which has difficulty finding room for forgiveness as a virtue. The ancient Greeks also had little or no use for this concept. Aristotle's famous description of the "great-souled" (or magnanimous) man can be found in his *Nicomachean Ethics* (1123b–1125b; all reputable editions of Aristotle use this numbering system). Aristotle clearly admires this man, but modern readers usually find this the portrait of a prig. Nietzsche was vehemently opposed to Christianity, with its emphasis on such traits as humility and forgiveness. Michael Ure's article, "The Politics of Mercy, Forgiveness and Love: A Nietzschean Appraisal" (2007), explains the outline of his view, but you may also want to look directly at a sample of Nietzsche's many writings. Dipping into *The Portable Nietzsche* (1977) will give you a general flavour, but you might also want to tackle *The Genealogy of Morals*, Nietzsche's most systematic work. His most sustained and scathing attack on Christian values comes in *The Anti-Christ*, the complete text of which is in *The Portable Nietzsche*.

Perhaps the most engaging and accessible introduction to the topic is provided by Jeffrie Murphy's *Getting Even* (2003). If you want to explore the issues Murphy raises in greater depth then he and Jean Hampton had a stimulating exchange in their important book *Forgiveness and Mercy* (1988). We comment in some detail on their discussion in our 2003 paper, "In Defence of Unconditional Forgiveness". Charles Griswold's *Forgiveness: A Philosophical Exploration* (2007) offers a more systematic and detailed discussion, including the history of the development of the idea that forgiveness is a virtue (for the ancient Greeks did not think it such).

We have said quite a lot in this book about the problem of forgiving atrocities, on which there is a rich literature. There are books by survivors, such as Améry, Lomax and Wiesenthal, as well as many books and papers reflecting on these dark episodes in human history. *Resentment's Virtue: Jean Améry and the Refusal to Forgive* by Thomas Brudholm (2008) and "Personal Relations and Moral Residue" by Eleonore Stump (2004) are very powerful, in their different ways, with Brudholm addressing serious problems raised by the advocacy of forgiveness, and Stump exploring the possibility that terrible wrongdoing leaves a "stain on the soul" of the perpetrator that may persist even where he has fully and genuinely repented.

Psychologists have done a lot of work in this area, as is reflected in this list. To get a good idea of what is going on we recommend starting with two websites: those of the American Psychological Association (www.apa.org) and the Forgiveness Institute (www.forgiveness-institute.org/index.htm). Sharon Lamb and Jeffrie Murphy's excellent collection of essays, *Before Forgiving: Cautionary Views of Forgiveness in Psychotherapy* (2002), casts a cool and slightly sceptical look at some of the more extravagant claims that have been made in this area.

American Psychological Association 2006 & 2008. "Forgiveness: A Sampling of Research Results", www.apa.org/international/resources/forgiveness.pdf (accessed July 2010).

Améry, J. 1980. *At the Mind's Limits*. Bloomington, IN: Indiana University Press.

Aristotle 1999. *Nicomachean Ethics*, T. Irwin (trans.). Indianapolis, IN: Hackett.

Bash, A. 2007. *Forgiveness and Christian Ethics*. Cambridge: Cambridge University Press.

Bowman, J. 2006. *Honor: A History*. New York: Encounter Books.

Brockaert, P. 1997. "The Negotiated Revolution: South Africa's Transition to a Multi-Racial Democracy". *Stanford Journal of International Law* **33**: 375–411.

Brudholm, T. 2008. *Resentment's Virtue: Jean Améry and the Refusal to Forgive*. Philadelphia, PA: Temple University Press.

Brudholm, T. & V. Rosoux 2009. "The Unforgiving: Reflections on Resistance to Forgiveness After Atrocity". *Law and Contemporary Problems* **72**: 33–49.

Butler, J. [1729] 1970. *Butler's Fifteen Sermons*. London: SPCK.

Diamond, J. 2008. "Abstract of 'Vengeance is Ours'". *New Yorker* (April).

Enright, R. D. & J. Rique 2004. *Enright Forgiveness Inventory*. Menlo Park, CA: Mind Garden.

Fincham, F. 2009. "Forgiveness: Integral to Close Relationships and Inimical to Justice". *Virginia Journal of Social Philosophy and the Law* **16**(2): 357–84. Available at www.chs.fsu.edu/~ffincham/pubs.html (accessed July 2010).

Freedman, S., R. D. Enright & J. Knutson 2005. "A Progress Report on the Process Model of Forgiveness". In *Handbook of Forgiveness*, E. L. Worthington (ed.), 393–406. New York: Routledge.

Garrard, E. 2002. "Forgiveness and the Holocaust". *Ethical Theory and Moral Practice* **5**(2): 147–65.

Garrard, E. & D. McNaughton. 2003. "In Defence of Unconditional Forgiveness". *Proceedings of the Aristotelian Society* **103**: 39–60.

Glover, J. 1999. *Humanity: A Moral History of the Twentieth Century*. London: Jonathan Cape.

Gourevitch, P. 2009 "Rwanda: Will the Truce Hold?" *The Observer* (8 November).

Griswold, C. 2007. *Forgiveness: A Philosophical Exploration.* Cambridge: Cambridge University Press.

Lamb, S. & J. G. Murphy. 2002. *Before Forgiving: Cautionary Views of Forgiveness in Psychotherapy.* Oxford: Oxford University Press.

Levi, P. 1986. *The Periodic Table.* London: Abacus.

Lewis, C. S. 1952. *Mere Christianity.* London: Fontana.

Lomax, E. 1995. *The Railway Man.* New York: Norton.

McMahan, J. 2009. *Killing in War.* Oxford: Oxford University Press.

McNulty, J. K. 2008. "Forgiveness in Marriage: Putting the Benefits into Context". *Journal of Family Psychology* **22** (1): 171–75.

Murphy, J. 2003. *Getting Even: Forgiveness and Its Limits.* Oxford: Oxford University Press.

Murphy, J. & J. Hampton 1988. *Forgiveness and Mercy.* Cambridge: Cambridge University Press.

Nietzsche, F. 1977. *The Portable Nietzsche,* W. Kaufmann (trans.) Harmondsworth: Penguin.

Nietzsche, F. 1994. *On the Genealogy of Morality,* C. Diethe (trans.). Cambridge: Cambridge University Press.

Rye, M., K. Pargament, M. Amir Ali *et al.* 2001. "Religious Perspectives on Forgiveness". In *Forgiveness: Theory, Research, and Practice,* M. E. McCullough, K. Pargament & C. Thoresen (eds), 17–40. New York: Guilford Press.

Seligman, M. & M. Csikszentmihalyi 2000. "Positive Psychology: An Introduction". *American Psychologist* **55**: 5–14.

Stump, E. 2004. "Personal Relations and Moral Residue". In *History of the Human Sciences: Theorizing from the Holocaust: What is to be Learned?,* P. Roth & M. S. Peacock (eds), **17** (2/3): 33–57.

Ure, M. 2007. "The Politics of Mercy, Forgiveness and Love: A Nietzschean Appraisal". *South African Journal of Philosophy* **26**(1): 55–68.

Wiesenthal, S. [1976] 1997. *The Sunflower.* New York: Shocken Books.

Index